Writing Outside the Lines

Writing Outside the Lines
Developing Partnerships
for Writers

Candida Gillis

Boynton/Cook Publishers
HEINEMANN
Portsmouth, NH

Boynton/Cook Publishers, Inc.
A subsidiary of Reed Elsevier Inc.
361 Hanover Street
Portsmouth, NH 03801-3912

Offices and agents throughout the world

The author and publisher wish to thank those who granted permission to reprint borrowed material:

"Fishing the Last Light" by Ron McFarland. In *Timberline* (Winter 1993). Reprinted by permission of the author and publisher.
"The Apology" by Ron McFarland. In *Tomorrow Magazine* (vol. 12, 1994). Reprinted by permission of the author and publisher.
"Encountering History in the Making" by Ron McFarland. Copyright © by Ron McFarland. Reprinted by permission of the author.
"Why I Love Baseball" by Ron McFarland. In Aethlon (vol. 13, 1995). Reprinted by permission of the author and publisher.
Excerpt from "If You Lose Your Pen" by Ruth Forman. From *We Are the Young Magicians* by Ruth Forman. Copyright © 1993 by Ruth Forman. Reprinted by permission of Beacon Press, Boston.

Library of Congress Cataloging-in-Publication Data
Gillis, Candida.
    Writing outside the lines: developing partnerships for writers/Candida Gillis.
      p. cm.
    ISBN 0-86709-422-2
    1. Creative writing (Elementary)—United States.   2. Creative writing (Secondary)—United States.   3. Mentoring in education—United States.
4. Community and school—United States.   I. Title.
LB1576.G4526   1997   97-4945
808'.042'0712—dc21   CIP

Editor: Peter R. Stillman
Manufacturing: Louise Richardson
Cover design: Judy Arisman
Back Cover photo of Candy Gillis and "Bishop" by Jackson Gillis Ludwig

Printed in the United States of America on acid-free paper

00 99 98 97 EB 1 2 3 4 5 6 7 8 9

To my son, Jackson, and the writer within

CONTENTS

ACKNOWLEDGMENTS

Thank you to the University of Idaho Department of English for its ongoing support of the Writing Partners Project and to the University for awarding me a sabbatical leave to prepare the materials for this book. My appreciation goes especially to the administrators and teachers in the Moscow School District. Their enthusiastic commitment to writing and to our community of writers provided the energy and encouragement to keep the project going. Thank you Alan Lee, Larry Verdal, Don Dempster, K. C. Albright, Susan Hodgin, Carolyn Tragesser, Pamela Wright, Carole Hughes, Elaine Jones, Doris Wear, Bart Quesnell, and Marcia Cooke. Thanks to Greg Branen for his assistance with the administrative details during the project's busiest time and to my son, Jackson, for acting as messenger. Most of all, thank you, writers. You are inspiring.

PREFACE

Writing Outside the Lines is the culmination of five years of work developing the Writing Partners Project, a project in which students in secondary and upper elementary schools who like to write form partnerships with older writers in the community. Partners share with each other and respond to work in progress, work completed, writing done for school, writing done at home—whatever they choose. I developed the project as a way to strengthen young peoples' identities as writers and deepen connections between school and community. The Writing Partners Project and this book came from my conviction that we are all writers at heart. We grow up playing with language—inventing, creating, composing. Without knowing it or consciously labeling ourselves, we are writers, yet some of us leave this unacknowledged identity behind when we go to school. A few abandon writing altogether; others are fortunate and, thanks to teachers who nourish the writer within, maintain the sense that writing is joyful.

This book is for all of you who want to help your students join that larger community of writers that exists beyond school. Herein are all the materials for establishing and running a program of writing partnerships. How and why I began the project and what I hoped younger and older writers would gain from exchanging writing are the subjects of Chapter 1. Chapter 2 explains how to get partnerships started—how to locate and enlist writers and organize the semester. When I talk at conferences about this project, teachers ask me whether I will send them the letters I use to explain the project to community writers, students, and their parents, the contracts writers sign, and more. All these are here. In Chapter 3, I focus on how to pair writers, how to pick up, deliver, and keep track of the exchanges, and how to deal with the inevitable problems. In the fourth chapter are suggestions for concluding the partnerships at the end of a semester, including tips for publishing an anthology, holding a reception, and planning the next round of partnerships. In the fifth chapter, I describe and illustrate some of the "results" of partnerships: what young writers and their parents see as the gains and how community writers view their experiences. Chapters 6 and 7 contain two case studies, of very different natures, that show what can happen over the course of a partnership—how writers react and respond to each other, how relationships develop. Throughout the book are many examples and illustrations from partners' writing; I think you will enjoy getting to know these writers as much as I have.

Please use this book: borrow the ideas and materials; change them to suit your needs or use them "as is." The book is my gift to you.

1
Becoming a Writer

Hello! My name is Jennifer. I consider myself a poet even though others
don't. Writing poetry is my favorite thing to do. Sometimes I get up in
the middle of the night and write so I won't forget my ideas. My brain
thinks poetry all day long and I find myself drifting away from classes to
think about poetry. I am hoping to become a writer. I'm not sure what
kind of writer yet but I still have a few years to think about it.

Jennifer, tenth grade

When I was growing up, I fell asleep to the sound of a typewriter. My father is a writer, and he often worked at home in a room not far from my bedroom. Late at night, as deadlines approached, I would hear him mutter
dialogue and hammer the keys. The typewriter's lullaby was mysterious and
awesome, for within its clack-a-clack were whole stories—pages of yellow
paper whose black, pica lines held characters and dramas that would one day
live on a television screen. During the day, in another corner of the house,
my mother, too, wrote. She kept a journal and wrote poetry, and though she
never published any (or tried to), her words were filled with music and magic
and seemed as important as those in any book.

In spite of such a verbal environment, I had no aspirations to become a
writer, although, in fact, I was one. My friends and I parodied, invented, and
reinvented every story that enchanted or annoyed us. We put new lyrics to
old songs, wrote skits, reenacted scenes from movies, told infinite jokes,
made up codes and messages, and dreamed scenarios for make-believe. Creating with language was for me, as it is for all children, an infinitely pleasurable game—a way to celebrate, define, experiment with, and judge the
world. What I did I never thought of as Real Writing. Real Writing was what
my father did—important, a little scary, and above all, hard work. I never
connected wordplay with serious writing (by definition writing was serious,
a notion I cannot shake even today). So a Real Writer was not what I wanted
to become when I grew up.

In school I was fortunate to have a few teachers who did not discourage
my pleasure; some inspired me. My fourth-grade teacher sponsored a play
writing contest with the winning play to be produced by the class (because it
was the only one that acknowledged the existence of real space and time and

a stage, mine won). My sixth-grade teacher's rather prolonged social studies unit sparked me to compose for extra credit an equally lengthy poem: "First we studied Mexico, It was long and very slow." With a few exceptions, school was another place where writing was structured, assigned "work." Back in the 1950s, writing was not a central part of school curriculum in my district. I remember much writing of spelling words in workbooks in elementary school, but except for the play and poem, I composed little besides thank-you letters for field trips, social studies reports, chapter outlines, or other exercises. In junior and senior high school, writing was mainly to explain what we had learned or to learn about paragraphs and practice sentences. Only in one English class were we asked to write creatively and expressively.

> For as long as I can remember, I have always loved to write, whether it be writing in a journal and letters to my friends or composing short stories, poems, and songs. When I was ten years old, I began writing by pretending that I was a journalist for a newspaper. I would make up articles about my family and the community and type them out on my grandmother's old typewriter. Then I would paste pictures of my family members beside the articles and have my mother photocopy my two-page "newspaper." I tried to sell them for five cents each, but only my immediate family members purchased them. I was proud of my accomplishments nonetheless. (Jill, college student)

Outside school I continued to take great pleasure in writing for fun. Like Jill, I once published a neighborhood newspaper on a hand-crank printing press set with rubber letters, but I was not a self-described journalist. I wrote poems in my head during the long walk home from school, although I shunned the title "poet." I, too, was proud of my accomplishments, giving writing as gifts and showing off to my parents or friends my creations. But it took me a long time to recognize that writing-for-play could be a serious endeavor and that being a writer was an exciting possibility. What it took for me was writing beyond myself, sharing my writing with a world larger than my family, best friend, or teachers, and a special gift that, in retrospect, changed my life.

My first real attempts to write "serious" stories for a real audience began when I was barely twelve and my family moved. I was separated from Barbara, my best friend and partner in wordplay. Cross-city calls were expensive in those days, so we wrote letters, missing each other and giggling on paper. Romantic, fantasy-filled teens, we decided she would write me a love story featuring me and some gorgeous guy, and I would in turn write one about her. I struggled with my story about her, for I had never tried to write a story before. To this day I have no idea what I wrote for her; I only remember wrestling with the story, and how childish mine seemed in comparison to the one she sent me. "Kisses That Clicked" was right out of the pages of *True Romance*, with its quick, witty narrative and realistic-sounding (to my twelve-year-old ear) dialogue. What amazed me most about Barbara's story was that it was told from the point of view of an older, wiser, more glamorous college girl. I was impressed beyond belief. That my friend, someone I knew who was my age, could write such a professional-sounding piece of prose was a revelation. Here was a real story, Real Writing, and Barbara had done it. Why couldn't I?

While my stories to and from Barbara helped me learn to think of myself as a writer, an even more significant influence was the gift of a portable electric typewriter. The machine became a marvelous machine for word-making. I spent hours freetyping to no one in particular, to a vaguely defined, fascinated (I imagined) audience eager to soak up every word I pecked out. I wrote nonsense, babbled in imaginary voices, and discovered a new way to express my chatty self. I had learned from Barbara that I could do in writing what I used to do with speech: I could become through my voice and language whoever I wanted to be. I could play with truth, be outrageous or silly, somber or dramatic; I could be far away or close up, here or there, myself or someone I wanted to become. What I had learned without knowing it was that I could do what authors do.

Out of my sessions on the typewriter emerged a short story that I sent to *American Girl*. I was thrilled when they sent me ten dollars and published it. Next, I wrote to Dick Clark's weekly advice-for-teens column in the Sunday newspaper magazine, and amazingly, several weeks later it appeared in the paper. At age fifteen, I had entered a world outside my small sphere; I belonged to a world of writers, and I finally dared to call myself one. Though I will never be entirely comfortable with the term, and though to this day I often cannot shake the image of the Real Writer as one who sweats away on the keys until dawn, I know that writing has always been and will always be a part of my life.

> I love to read and write, but I often don't have much time to do either. Most of the writing I do is for assignments, and I occasionally write poetry on my own. One thing I do often is write in my journal and have succeeded to keep it fairly updated. (Hannah, eighth grade)

In many classrooms today, young people are treated as authors from the moment they hold pencils. In workshop settings, teachers write with their students and share the agonies and joys of being writers. Nancie Atwell writes, "From the first day of school I expect [my students will] participate in written language as real writers and real readers do—as I do—and I promise what we do together will make sense and bring satisfaction" (49). In classes like Atwell's, young writers do everything seasoned writers do; they mull over ideas, draft, confer, revise, redraft, and publish. They have time to write in an atmosphere that invites and encourages writing, with teacher-writers who help them discover how writing gives shape and meaning to their lives and worlds. These students are learning to trust and have faith in the writer within. I envy children today who learn in schools that writing is a natural part of themselves, for I suspect that they will grow up not only relishing the playfulness of writing but also more able to deal with the struggles and setbacks writers sometimes endure. To this day, my identity as a writer is fragile. As I sit before the computer screen silently mumbling sentences that I will soon commit to print, I wonder what my life would be like had I been taught by teachers influenced by Nancie Atwell or Lucy Calkins, Donald Graves or Peter Elbow, writers who have helped so many teachers nurture the writers inside each of their students.

Teachers play a large part in helping children see themselves as writers. When the classroom becomes an authentic learning community in which writing is integral, children have a greater sense of their own power with language than when they write in isolation and *for* (rather than with) the teacher. In many classrooms today, students collaborate in all stages of writing and write for audiences that include not only their classmates and families, but their nearer or larger communities as well. Publishing may go far beyond the classroom bulletin board or anthology. Students publish books of community and family history, "how-to" and storybooks for school libraries, text for local merchants' advertising, collections of poetry, film reviews and essays for newspapers, and more. A useful book for all writing teachers, *Classroom Publishing,* edited by Laurie King and Dennis Stoval describes some creative projects that teachers across the United States have undertaken, including multilingual books of folk tales and poetry, books for children in Nicaragua, ethnographies, anthologies of writing by students in correctional facilities, and science and art magazines. The old toy printing press has given way to computers that make classroom publishing easier and more exciting.

> Shirley Brice Heath has gone so far as to suggest that the single most important condition for literary learning is the presence of mentors who are joyfully literate people. (148)

For a long time, people thought of writing as an activity that separated the writer from the community. Jo March writing her fiction in isolation from her family, the starving artist in the garret, even my father late at night: these are images that still pervade our culture. As I was growing up and even into the 1970s, when I taught high school and then became a graduate student, school writing was largely an individual endeavor, separate writers at separate desks. Although the workshop approach to writing instruction is changing our notion of writing from an act of lonely toil to a process of collaboration, and students today are encouraged to think of themselves as writers at early ages, the shadow of the writer as isolate still exists. Many young people grow up with the notion that their writing is interesting only to a limited audience of teachers, parents, or friends, if anyone. And some feel "weird," different, and have no inkling that other kindred spirits exist in their schools and communities. I knew one adolescent who was thoroughly convinced that no one in her school could possibly understand her poetry, and certainly, that no one else shared her love of the craft. I am sure she was not alone in her feelings. Young writers like her are surprised to learn that others of different ages, interests, and backgrounds also love to write and would take pleasure in reading their work. If being a writer depends on having genuine audiences in nonschool settings, students must somehow enter into that larger writing community. They must write outside the lines that separate schools from the worlds in which they live.

> . . . as human beings we write to communicate, plan, petition, remember, announce, list, imagine. . . but above all, we write to hold our lives in our hands and to make something out of them. (Calkins, 8)

It comes as a happy surprise to many young writers that so many people of all ages enjoy writing whether they publish or not. For many of us, writing is a way of responding to life. We are a society of journal keepers, letter writers, political editorialists, private poets. We write feelings, opinions, ideas, stories, and laws. We persuade, affirm, assert, inform, plead, argue, praise, insult, preach, and eulogize. Through language, and specifically through writing, we participate in our society and its government. Whether we write for work or as a pastime, incidentally or obsessively, we are connected to each other by our word-making. Young writers, who, as I did, write for play and pleasure share much with all of us who write, for we all struggle to find the right words to fit our passions or politics and find intense pleasure when someone responds exactly the way we want.

Dear Writing Partner,

I am delighted to be involved in this writing project, and looking forward to hearing from you. First off here are a few facts about me. I am a seventy two year old Granma, have lived here in Moscow for fourteen (14) years. My interests are, of course *writing*! Music—I play the harmonica, and have a keyboard which I also play. I have not had music lessons, so this is all done by ear (that always sounded strange to me to say "by ear" when what

I actually use are my hands and, of course, my mouth for the harmonica).
I am involved with the Senior Citizens, having been one for lo! these
many years. I grew up in Deerfield, Illinois, the Chicago area, moved to
Calif. in 1948 and raised my family there. I love animals, have two cats—
very intelligent critters and much beloved by my husband and me. I like
children, sports, the desert, the ocean, fall weather, first snowfalls, cook-
ing, good discussions, but my first love is *poetry* and rhyming— there is always some rhyme bouncing around in my head waiting to be typed or
written. We have a motor home, and sometimes travel in it—that's exciting! Perhaps this is too lengthy an introduction, so will say no more, until I hear from you, my Writing Partner.

Sincerely,
Bette

I developed the Writing Partners Project as a way to strengthen young
writers' identities as writers and to help them discover and participate in the
community of writers outside their school. The idea is quite simple: by sharing writing with an older writer in the community and, in turn, by reading
and responding to that person's writing, a student who likes to write learns
that his writing is worthwhile and interesting to another, older writer—
someone outside the classroom and family. In addition, he discovers that all
writers regardless of age engage in similar processes while writing, share similar struggles and successes. He learns that he can be a helpful reader to another writer, and that he can see his own writing in new ways. I call the
project Writing Partners because that is what those who participate become—partners who exchange, read, and enjoy each others' work for a period of time. I have been running my Writing Partners Project for the last
five years, and every year I learn a little bit more about how to make it more
efficient and rewarding and I become more committed to the value of the
project for young and older writers alike.

Students can exchange their writing with people outside the classroom
in various ways, most recently on the Internet. In the October 1995 issue of
the *English Journal*, three teachers describe their experiments and adventures
using computer technology to help their students acquire audiences outside
the classroom. In "A Journey through Cyberspace: Reading and Writing in
a Virtual School," Harry Noden describes how his students send writing to
other classes, post their writing on electronic bulletin boards, and respond
to the writing of others. Chris Davis' students exchange writing with other
classes across the country via e-mail Donald Graves' students use America
Online's writing exchange program, Scrapbook USA. Less technologically
oriented exchanges include programs like Writing Buddies, in which older

senior or junior high writers share writing with or help to mentor younger students, interschool pen-pal exchanges, and community-based programs in which students help elders or others in the community produce books or newsletters (see Gillis, 1992). What gives Writing Partners its power is precisely its simplicity. Requiring no computers, Internet access, or field trips outside the school, it brings together young writers with people in the same community in an impersonal yet intimate way. School-community partners have no common bond but their love of writing and their geographical proximity. Their connection is solely to share their work-in-progress and to seek advice from each other in a nonthreatening environment. Although they do not meet until the end of the semester, they get to know each other through writing. And all writers may participate, even those without computers. (A community of writers includes everyone who writes, not merely the technologically privileged.) While there is much value in belonging to a global community, there is equal value in strengthening ties with one's local community and in discovering the richness that it holds.

Dear Writing Partner,

Greetings. My name is Abby. I am a poet (I just finished my M.F.A., which means I got to write poetry for two years after college and they gave me a degree for it!) and also a teacher.

Writing poetry, being a poet is the most important thing in the world to me. I saw a bumper sticker the other day—"create senseless acts of beauty"—and I thought, yes, that's what writing means to me. It doesn't make much money, it's not always appreciated by bunches of people, but it's creating something beautiful. And by beautiful, I don't mean that you have to write about beautiful things. I often write about the "ugly" side of life, but when you write a poem about it, it creates something that is beautiful also. Does that make sense?

The poem I am sending you is about my mother-in-law. She went blind when she was in her twenties. I put the poem in her voice (I pretended I was her) because I thought it would make the emotional scene more immediate. I hope you like it.

I am really looking forward to corresponding with you and reading what you are working on. I think you'll find that one of the best parts about being a writer is being part of a writing community. We write alone, but it's always wonderful to share the work with others.

When I began Writing Partners, I had several goals in mind, though at first my intent was twofold: 1) to bring a wider audience of readers to students in the junior and senior high who love to write; and 2) to bring the writing of local adolescents to the students in my college course on the theory and practice of teaching writing. A third goal for the project took shape after the project's maiden year: to give writers in the community the chance to connect with younger writers, to write outside *their* lines, and see how imaginative and creative young people can be. Ultimately, I hoped the partnerships would build a stronger community.

At the project's outset, I was (and still am) convinced that by exchanging writing with a writer in the college and community over a period of months, young authors would not only receive more encouragement and support, but also gain a greater sense of the rhetorical nature of their writing—the context, the audience, the purpose. By having to explain to someone outside the school setting what a piece of writing is *for*, what it is trying to do, a writer becomes more conscious of her intent. And she must take the piece seriously; it is no longer something scribbled off in response to an assignment but has a purpose, is designed to affect a reader in some way. The poem is about a friend, a feeling, a response to an event, a book; it is meant to make the reader feel the horror of battle, understand the poet's loss, know her anger or joy. In addition, by seeing how a partner responds, a writer can learn how her writing affects an audience other than teacher or peer. What parts are especially engaging? What works? What does not? The questions the older partner asks can give the author ideas about feedback she herself might seek and how she might read her own work with a more critical eye. In other words, I hoped that partnerships would foster greater reflection about writing, the understanding that writers continually fine-tune their work to achieve desired effects, the ability to formulate questions about one's own writing, and the ability to respond thoughtfully.

I also hoped young writers would benefit by their exposure to different types of writing—new subjects, new forms, new styles—and, simultaneously, by the discovery that they have things in common with people of other ages and experiences. The young writer who thinks poetry should rhyme has a partner dedicated to unrhymed free verse. A nature essayist meets an editorial writer, a fiction writer helps a partner struggle with autobiography, one who dwells on the serious is paired with a comic, a romance lover reads war stories. Older writers can give the younger ones new slants on history, community, family, and life in general. And young writers can discover what entertaining, thought-provoking, engaging treasures exist in their own backyards, written by real people in their neighborhoods, towns, cities—treasures perhaps just as interesting as what lies between the covers of a book or on a teacher's handout. Despite their differences in age and experience, partners can share a love of writing and a writer's way of viewing the world. All writers are in the business of shaping experience and seek ways to do that more effectively. Therefore, they have a language with which to communicate about their craft, and they use this language to encourage and assist each other. As fellow writers, partners can appreciate each others' struggles and give suggestions that are sometimes taken more seriously than if given by a teacher or a classmate, perceived as "someone who does not understand because he is not a writer."

A central premise of Writing Partners exchanges is that the older writers not play roles of teacher or editor unless the partner asks. I envisioned partners as co-writers, and the senior partner's role as that of an articulate, encouraging reader—not an absolute authority on writing, but someone with more experience and perhaps knowledge of how to talk about writing—whose job it is to answer the young writer's questions and respond honestly and supportively. For a partnership to help a young writer establish a writerly identity, partners must perceive themselves as somewhat equal in their status as writers and respond to each other's writing accordingly. In the world outside school, writers seek advice from other writers; younger writers, however, are used to viewing adults as authorities, and although they look to fellow writers for advice, they take more seriously advice from teachers (who, after all, give the grades). I hoped that because the older partners would not be associated with school, they would have a different kind of authority—the kind one gives a co-worker, a colleague in a senior or more experienced rank. This person is not the boss but one who "has been there and knows the ropes." Or, perhaps, the older partner would seem not an authority at all but a co-worker: "we're in this together; how do *you* do it?"

Peter Elbow once wrote that one benefit of sharing writing is the writer's "sense of feasibility."

> But then along comes that really good passage written by someone like you. It's not unbelievably good, indeed what's special is its believability: it's mixed in with other passages that are quite ordinary; it even has some obvious weaknesses. But it is so good that it makes you positively hungry to hear more, makes you wish you had written it, and then finally, makes you realize that you *could* have written it. (23)

By reading their partners' writing—sometimes polished sometimes not, sometimes successful sometimes not, sometimes complete sometimes in progress—young writers can see reflections of themselves, imperfections that make their own struggles seem a natural part of the writing process. Because many older writers are not professional, younger writers can glimpse the importance of writing throughout life. Not all people who love to write are greatly skilled or published; not all writers want to publish for anyone other than friends or family. Yet all take pleasure in the process and are gratified by a product that evokes a favorable response in the reader. Writing is a life-long pleasure for so many people, yet it does not always come easily; writers of all ages sometimes have doubts, questions, insecurities, in addition to fun. This knowledge is important for young writers.

I hoped that older writers, too, would benefit from having younger partners. They could become better acquainted with adolescents and the kind of writing they like to do and perhaps be inspired with new ideas for their own work. When I initially talked to writers to assess their interest in becoming writing partners, I learned that many would welcome the opportunity to work with younger writers though they were unfamiliar with their writing. Many adults are surprised that people so young can write rich, fluent, and imaginative pieces (despite an occasional absence of technical skill). Even work that seems trite or shallow from an adult perspective has a vitality and sincerity that most older writers find engaging, if not familiar from their own youth. I hoped that because they are people for whom writing is a part of their lives, older partners could encourage this commitment through their enthusiasm and genuine interest in their partners' writing. Conversely, I hoped that the writing of young people could give older writers an opportunity to appreciate their youthful partners' energy and visions and, most of all, their enthusiasm for writing. When people who are separated by age or other factors discover common interests, our communities benefit. Writing is not enjoyed exclusively by a community's elite or by the young, old, male, female, "A" student, drop-out, professional, or unemployed. It is an endeavor that gives pleasure to everyone and unites all who do it.

My college students likewise could gain much from partnerships. They could learn more about young people and their writing, and also have a chance to practice responding as readers, not instructors. Although the texts in my course are loaded with examples of young peoples' writing, my students are not able to see firsthand the variety of writing of students in local schools. Our community is small, and "field experience" is limited to classes later in their preparation. I wanted my students to witness young writers' enthusiasm, learn what subjects (and the diversity!) teens like to write about, and get a feel for the range of language fluency and rhetorical control. In addition, having partners would mean being writers themselves, aware of their own processes and insecurities, willing to take ownership of their work, and more conscious of the contexts and purposes of their own writing. It would mean learning to formulate questions about their writing, and being willing to examine its strengths and weaknesses.

Having a partner would also give my teachers-to-be the opportunity to respond positively, constructively, enthusiastically, sensitively, and appreciatively. Many preservice teachers tend to wear the authority hat once they are in the presence of young peoples' writing; the idea that they can read a fourteen-year-old's poem or a sixteen-year-old's story for pleasure is unfamiliar. Yet to be effective teachers, they must learn to read as readers first, before they read as editors or evaluators. They need learn to imagine, when they read their students' writing, that they are home in a comfortable chair, not thinking about teaching or instructing, but indulging in the pleasure of a good read—feet propped up, a steaming cup of something delicious nearby, with no pens or pencils handy. Having a partner would help my students practice reading for pleasure, personal enrichment, delight.

These, then became my goals for Writing Partners:

For young writers:

- to extend the audience for writing beyond the teacher, parents, peers
- to provide additional positive responses to their writing and encouragement to continue writing
- to expose young writers to new writing ideas, subjects, and genres, and to stimulate experimentation and risk-taking
- to encourage thoughtful response to others' writing
- to encourage young writers to solicit responses to their own writing and therefore reflect on their own intentions and strategies
- to encourage self-reflection and assessment of their own writing processes, goals, and accomplishments
- to introduce writers to the processes in which older, often more experienced writers engage
- to show younger writers that writing can be a life-long, rewarding endeavor
- to enable younger writers to feel part of the larger community of writers outside the school

For older writers:

- to increase familiarity with the interests and concerns of young people in the community
- to stimulate and enrich their own writing
- to offer a chance for reflection on the process of writing

- to encourage an appreciation for the efforts, strengths, and abilities of younger writers

For preservice teachers:

- to learn some of the kinds of writing assignments made in classes and the kinds of writing students do in and out of school
- to provide experience in responding positively to writing and an opportunity to practice responding as readers first, and supportive critics when asked
- to build excitement about the teaching of writing and working with young writers

Above all, I designed Writing Partners to help all writers share their enthusiasm for and appreciation of the diverse and rewarding endeavor of writing and to inspire writers at all levels. Writing is a habit, a passion, a pleasure worth nurturing. For the most part, the partnerships between student and community writers that I, and the teachers who worked with me, established over the last five years met or exceeded my expectations. I am convinced beyond a doubt that partnerships can be a rich experience for everyone. In the chapters that follow, I explain the mechanics of setting up and running a partnership project, including the problems I encountered, the strategies I learned, and some of the benefits that resulted from partnerships since I began the project in 1992. I hope you will be encouraged to begin partnerships of your own.

2
Setting Up a
Writing Partners Program

Dear Student,

Do you like to write? Are you a poet, a writer of stories? Do you like to write memories, letters, essays? If so, you might like to participate in the Writing Partners Project. You don't need to be a "great" writer to join; all you need is to enjoy writing and sharing your work with another writer.

In a nutshell, here is how Writing Partners works: partners exchange writing for one semester. One semester is an ideal time frame for the exchange of writing because it allows writers to change partners if they wish or to drop out of the program if other commitments take precedence. Because junior and senior high students sometimes change English classes at semester, they may be hard to track down, making a year-long exchange of writing complicated. During the semester, students and community writers exchange and respond to each others' writing approximately once every two weeks (described in Chapter 3). At the end of the semester, as a culminating activity, my college students and I produce an anthology of partners' writing and host a reception for the partners to meet and celebrate their writing. (These activities and variations are described in Chapter 4.) However, establishing what may appear to be a simple exchange requires some work: locating and enlisting community and student writers, soliciting cooperation of administrators, informing and obtaining permission from students' parents, organizing and administrating the exchanges, and more. In this chapter, I describe the nuts and bolts of starting partnerships, including the strategies and materials that can help you inform the participants and safeguard yourself, the writers, and your school. Setting up a Writing Partners program is complicated, but I have done most of it for you. Here is an overview of the tasks that may be necessary in an entire semester of Writing Partners. Do not be discouraged by the quantity of detail; I find that the more organized and prepared I am, the more smoothly the project runs.

Writing Partners Semester Timeline

Before the semester begins:

- Prepare sets of materials for students, community writers, parents, teachers.
- Obtain approval from appropriate building principals, department heads, and teachers.
- Solicit interest from writers in the community, including college students, other teachers.
- Solicit funding, if possible, for the production of the anthology.
- Send materials to prospective community writers.
- Collect signed "Community Writing Partners' Responsibilities" forms and introductory "Dear Writing Partner" letters from community writers.

At semester's beginning:

- Distribute materials to interested students.
- Collect signed parent permit slips and signed "Student Writing Partners' Responsibilities" contracts from students.
- Pair community writers with students.
- Create a master list of writing partners.
- Make arrangements for end-of-semester reception (reserve room, etc.), and set due dates for submissions to the anthology.

During the semester:

- Manage the exchange of writing (through drop-off/pick-up envelopes, the mail, personal delivery).
- Keep track of students who are behind, and make partner substitutions if someone drops out. Send reminders or call partners late in responding.
- Make decisions about editors for anthology, format, and so forth.
- Send early announcements of reception date to community writers.

Late in the semester:

- Send announcements to all partners about the anthology, including deadlines.
- Receive submissions from partners and prepare (or have students or editors prepare) camera-ready copy.

- Have editors do layout, and determine the exact cost per anthology; bargain hunt for inexpensive copying.
- Take orders for anthologies.
- Collect orders and money from partners; have anthologies printed.
- Arrange for snacks for the reception.
- Distribute project evaluation forms for all participants.
- Send "formal" invitations to the reception.
- Distribute evaluation forms.

Finally:

- Attend the reception where editors distribute anthologies; collect the evaluation forms. Enjoy!
- Prepare for the next semester.

So let's begin at the beginning, with the work that needs to be done before the start of the semester.

Engaging Partners in the Community

When I initiated the Writing Partners Project, I began simply, working in collaboration with two eighth-grade teachers. The community writers consisted of college students in my course, Writing Workshop for Teachers, and they exchanged writing with student volunteers in the two teachers' English classes. That first year I learned an enormous amount about managing the interchange of writing, and the project was extremely time-consuming. But in later years, after many experiments, headaches, and bungles, the kinks disappeared. As the project grew in reputation and became easier to run, I was able to expand it to include writers in the community; the number of participants grew. More teachers requested partners for their students, and more students wanted to participate than we could find partners for. In one semester, here is what the writers in the project looked like:

PARTICIPANTS IN WRITING PARTNERS, FALL '94

Writers in the Community:

- twenty-three college students in a composition methods course
- seven college students in advanced writing courses
- two newspaper reporters
- one writer for a university news service
- two tenured, full-time university teachers (one a published nature writer and the other a published poet, literary scholar, and editor of poetry anthologies)

- two homemakers and part-time teachers
- one secretary and author of technical manuals and poetry
- one "farm hand-construction worker-cabinet maker-business owner-Union representative-millwright and finally retiree in that order"

Writers in the Schools:

- thirty-three students in grades eight and nine
- ten students in grades ten and eleven
- eighteen students in grades five and six

Selecting Writers

A key element of Writing Partners exchanges is that they be voluntary. School and community writers must want to participate and feel comfortable sharing their writing with a complete stranger. They need not be great writers, professionals, published, nor do the student writers need to excel in writing to participate. In fact, many of the students who want partners are not the best writers in the class. Partners should be people who love to write, write regularly, and enjoy sharing their writing with others. In addition, they should be responsible enough to read and respond thoughtfully to the writing they receive.

When I was developing Writing Partners, I thought advertising in a local newspaper would be a good way to locate interested writers. I was warned away from doing this by an astute principal rightfully concerned about potential risk to students by not carefully screening writers who participate. I am grateful for his advice. Not all writers write material appropriate for young readers, and some screening is required to ensure the students' safety and to protect the teachers and schools. So I developed these guidelines for selecting community writers:

GUIDELINES FOR SELECTION OF COMMUNITY WRITING PARTNERS

To participate in the Writing Partners Project and be a writing partner to a student in elementary, junior, or senior high school, a person must be

1. a member of the community who
   a. writes regularly for personal pleasure or professionally
   b. writes nonfiction, fiction, or poetry suitable both in content and form for sharing with a young writer
   c. shares or has shared writing with others regularly through membership in a writing group, workshop or class, or through publication
   d. has provided a character reference

   OR

2. a university student who is currently or recently enrolled in a writing methods class or another upper-level writing course *and* has had demonstrated experience with young people (through teaching, camp counseling, enrollment in a program leading toward teacher certification, etc.)

In addition, all participating community writers must sign the Community Writing Partners' Responsibilities form and provide a character reference.

These guidelines, along with the contract described later ("Community Writing Partners' Responsibilities"), assure school administrators and parents that the partners selected are serious writers interested in working with young people and used to sharing writing publicly.

One issue in writer selection that arose initially was whether the writers' work would be appropriate for young readers. I did not request a sample of writing from prospective writers because ours is a small town and the writers I encounter are either known to me or recommended by someone who knows their work. In a larger community, if I had a large number of writers whose work I did not know, I would ask for a sample of writing. But the project is not designed solely for writers who write for adolescents or children. In my projects, I have had writers who wrote fairly sophisticated fiction, poetry, and essays for adult readers that clearly went "over the heads" of their partners, yet this did not seem to lessen the young writers' interests in their partnerships. Sometimes young writers feel flattered to be included as audience for more mature writing. (I discuss the issue of appropriateness further in Chapter 3.)

Related to the issue of appropriateness was the issue of correctness. What about writers whose command of conventions of usage, punctuation, syntax, or spelling was not perfect? On the one hand, I wanted young writers to read exemplary writing, but on the other, I felt they should see real writing by real people that might be less than correct by publishing standards. The teachers and I concurred that the benefits of reading nonacademic writing by community residents outweighed the risk of exposure to misspellings and comma faults. They saw a genuine advantage in students' seeing imperfect drafts, particularly those not published or in progress. We agreed that, as a policy, lack of correctness would not keep a writer from participating, although I do ask writers to send material that is "proofread and legible." This policy is especially applicable to writers who may not use computers. Ralph, my oldest partner, whose writing appears throughout this book and especially in Chapter 7, writes on a manual typewriter. His writing is full of typos (for which he regularly apologizes to his partners), yet his writing is rich and entertaining, and I would not allow surface errors to prevent his writing from being enjoyed by younger readers.

Locating Writers

Our community is small, yet I was surprised by how many writers I located once I began digging around. Writers are everywhere:

- Check with faculty of local schools and colleges. In our local junior and senior high are several teachers (not all of them English teachers) who write. In the university, writers abound, not merely in English departments but among campus staff as well. Teachers in the district who have participated in National Writing Project summer sessions and workshops are ideal candidates. You might even find writers from the ranks of administration.
- Ask friends and colleagues. I found several writers by asking friends— everyone knows someone who writes. Ralph is the father of a friend; others are friends of friends.
- Check local libraries, churches, and seniors' centers for existing writing workshop groups that meet regularly to share writing (I found one partner in an elders' writing group). Also, ask members of local poetry or books clubs.
- Visit local newspaper or journal offices and ask reporters, feature writers, even editors. Most journalists are enthusiastic about supporting community writing.
- Ask writers themselves. Writers often have a network of other writers and gladly pass along names of people they think would enjoy exchanging writing with a student writer. I regularly receive recommendations from writers who have participated in earlier projects.
- Ask parents. I ask parents of the younger writers at the end of the semester if they or someone they know would like to have a partner in the future.
- Call English departments in local colleges and universities. Some students in upper-level writing classes or in education classes, particularly students interested in becoming teachers and/or who have worked with adolescents or children, may be interested. I discovered several student partners in classes other than my writing methods class who became enthusiastic and responsible partners for several semesters. (One caution: check first to make sure the student writes material that is appropriate for young readers.)

Initial Meetings With Writers

In order to interest a writer in participating in the project, I meet or speak with her to explain the nature of the project and give an overview of what her participation will entail. I stress the goals of the project, the value of the partnerships for the young writers, and possible gains for the older writers. I also stress that their participation requires only a little time and work and that the nature of the project is nonjudgmental; they are simply to read and enjoy their partners' writing and to take pleasure in the writing sent to them. I reassure them that they are not signing on as tutors or specialists, but merely as people in the community who like to write and who want to share their writing with other, younger, writers. I have found that writers who have not worked with young people tend to have similar questions and concerns. It helps to be prepared, when speaking with prospective community writers, with as much information as possible about what they can expect. Here are the FAQs, the most Frequently Asked Questions by community writers, and the kinds of answers I generally give:

Question: How much time will my participation take?

Answer: Not much, depending on your partner—how much and how regularly your partner writes. Some young writers write only a short, sometimes dashed-off piece, maybe a paragraph or short poem. Other writers write five-page short stories or essays. Some writers write quite fluently; others are struggling. Generally, you should respond to your partner's writing and send writing of your own no later than two weeks after you receive writing, so you have plenty of time.

Question: Do I have to send new writing to my partner? I don't write regularly, and I'm not working on anything now.

Answer: No. You may send work previously written or work in progress. Young writers appreciate seeing "unfinished" pieces, especially when you also ask for their advice. But if you aren't currently writing, an earlier piece is just fine. [I have learned that some elder writers and non-professionals are concerned about producing new writing every two weeks.]

Question: How much writing do I send?

Answer: Again, this may depend on your partner. If your partner is a fluent writer and is sending you lengthy pieces, you should feel comfortable sending whatever length work you like. However, I generally recommend no more than three pages. Students have other work, and if you send too much, they might not have time to read and respond. Too much writing can have the effect of overwhelming an inexperienced writer. A good strategy is to begin by sending one, shorter piece and asking the partner if she or he would like to have more.

Question: Will a young writer be interested in my work?

Answer: Usually, you are paired with a young writer based on mutual interest in type of writing (poetry, fiction, etc.) or in what you like to write about, but sometimes this isn't possible. Expect surprises. I tell students that you, like them, are writers with subjects and projects of your own, and that the value of the partnership is to learn the kinds of writing other people do and how to help another writer accomplish his goals. Send writing *you* find interesting and tell your partner why. In most cases, your partner will be interested because you are interested, and your partner will respect that. [People working on family history and memoirs are especially concerned that young writers will have no interest in their material and need reassurance. In my work with elder writers, I found that some may not see their lives as inherently interesting to anyone outside their families. Many young people, however, are curious about the past and find reading their partners' memory writing entertaining. Explaining this to older writers may encourage them to share their work with younger partners.]

Question: How will I help a younger writer?

Answer: You help simply by reading and responding to your partner's writing and by giving him or her some writing of your own. Your role is not one of tutor but of fellow writer. As such, you do not correct or teach, although you may give constructive suggestions. If your partner asks a specific question, answer it honestly. Otherwise, respond by being supportive and positive. [I provide community writers with a handout on "Responding to Your Partner's Writing," given in Chapter 3.]

Question: How much response do I give? How much can I expect?

Answer: Generally, a good rule of thumb is to answer all questions your partner asks, and tell what you liked about his or her writing. A paragraph is plenty. You may have a partner who wants detailed response and criticism (not likely); in that case, provide more. Be cautious of responding in too much detail so as not to overwhelm a writer, or in too little. Best ask the partner how much and what kind of response he or she would like. In terms of what to expect from your younger partner, some respond very little while others say quite a lot. Do not expect an extensive response. A short response does not necessarily mean that your partner has not read or enjoyed your writing; some readers are better than others at describing what they like in a piece of writing. Others are quite articulate and go into great depth. The maturity of your partner, his or her experience as a writer, and the workload will determine how much your partner says. At times in the semester, particularly toward the end, your partner will be very busy and will likely say less.

I often do not go into much detail during these initial meetings, in which my main goal is to entice the writers into becoming partners, but questions like these are almost always asked. You will see that much of the foregoing information is repeated in materials that I send the writers later, once they decide to participate, but it helps to be prepared during the first meeting. If I talk with writers in person, I bring samples of young partners' writing and letters to illustrate the program. If I speak on the phone, I offer to send samples along with my follow-up material.

The Follow-up: "Dear Writer" Letters and Contracts

Once I have talked with writers about the project, I follow up my meeting with a "Dear Writer" letter that explains in more detail the nature of the program and the community writer's responsibilities. The letter also provides dates and other information about the upcoming semester. Here is an example of a letter I have used:

> Dear Writer,
>
> Thank you for your interest in participating in the Writing Partners Project. The project requires only a little of your time and work; yet it can be very rewarding. As a writing partner, you will be paired with a student in the junior or senior high school who enjoys writing and would like to exchange writing with a writer in the Moscow community. By sharing some of your writing with your partner and by responding to his or her material, you can encourage and support a young writer's efforts, help him or her feel part of a larger community of writers, and show that writing can be a lifelong pleasure.
>
> Your participation will be for one university semester. (If you would like to participate again in the next semester's project, you will have that opportunity.) Here is what you do to participate this semester:
>
> 1. *Read and sign the "Community Writing Partners' Responsibilities" form* included in the packet of materials attached.
> 2. *Write a brief introductory letter* for your partner telling something about yourself, what you like to write, etc. The letter may be hand written but should be proofread and legible. Begin the letter "Dear Writing Partner." A sample letter is attached.
> 3. *Attach to your letter a copy of some of your writing* that you would like to share with your partner. It may be writing you have done recently or in the past, or writing you are currently working on. It may be handwritten or typed, but should be appropriate for a young reader, and proofread and legible (see "Community Writing Partners'

Responsibilities"). Keep the length to two pages. In your letter, you might provide the reader with a context for the writing—what prompted you to write it, what you were trying to accomplish, what you plan to do next (if the writing is incomplete). Include any questions you might like your partner to answer, for example, "I'm not satisfied with the end. Do you have any ideas?" or "What do you think is the most convincing part?" You might ask your reader to suggest a direction, add an ending, chapter, or verse. Or you may simply want to ask your reader to enjoy your piece. Keep a copy of your writing. Your partner will be instructed to return your writing, but you'd be wise to keep a copy just in case he or she forgets.

4. *Return your signed "Community Writers' Responsibilities" form, along with your introductory "Dear Writing Partner" letter and writing for your partner, to me.* Either mail it to me at the English Department or phone me, and I or my assistant will stop by your house or office and pick it up. [My phone numbers go here.] I would like your initial material as soon as possible. Once I receive your form and writing, the teachers and I will make sure that you are assigned a partner (if you have an age preference, please let me know). Once your partner receives your letter and writing, he or she will have a week to write a letter and send some writing back. When I have writing from your partner, I will deliver or mail it to you. After you receive your partner's letter and writing, you should write a short response and send more of your own writing in no more than two weeks (also, return the writing your partner sent). Your responses need not be lengthy, but should be positive and encouraging. I will send you ideas about how to respond to your partners' writing soon.

At the end of the semester, my Writing Workshop for Teachers class will produce an anthology of writing partners' writing. You will be asked to submit something, as will all participants in the project. Also, during the week of _____, we will host a reception so that you and your partner can meet. Details about the anthology and reception will come later.

If you have any questions on your role as a writing partner, let me know. I will be in touch with you during the semester. And thank you very much!

Sincerely,
Candida Gillis, Project Director

This letter outlines the basic structure of the program. A "Community Writers' Responsibilities" form is attached to the letter as a kind of contract that ensures that the writer has read and understood her or his responsibilities and role. (I sometimes follow up the letter and form with a phone call, to make sure the partner understands and to answer any questions or concerns.)

The contract provides a certain degree of protection for the teacher or whoever is running Writing Partners, by making it clear that participants receive no remuneration or other tangible benefit, and that they may end their participation at any time. I have also used this contract as a release form, enabling me to quote from the writer's work in presentations and publications. I also ask for the name and phone number of a character reference, in addition to information about the writer that can help teachers pair writers with their students. Other statements on the form clarify the nature of the relationship the writer will have with the student; they were designed for reasons discussed later in this chapter.

COMMUNITY WRITING PARTNERS' RESPONSIBILITIES

Participating partners please read, sign, answer the questions on the bottom of the page, and return to the project director.

As a participant in the Writing Partners Project I promise that I will

1. send, through the project director, some of my original writing to my partner at least every two weeks and communicate with my partner solely for the purpose of sharing and responding to writing.
2. send writing that is of suitable content for my younger partner and in a form that is polished and legible and uses conventions of standard publishing English.
3. give my partner written comments about his or her writing that are helpful and supportive and answer any questions my partner has asked about his or her writing.
4. return my partner's writing and my comments about it in a timely fashion.
5. notify the project director immediately if I wish to discontinue the program.

I understand that

1. the aim of the program is to help participants appreciate and enjoy writing, and that my role as a writing partner is to be supportive and encouraging.
2. if I have problems with the program I may freely share my concerns with the project director.
3. if I do not respond to and send writing regularly, I may be asked to discontinue the program.
4. all writing and letters to my partner will go through the project director and my partner's English teacher; likewise, all writing from my partner will come through the director and teacher.
5. the director and my partner's teacher may read the writing and letters I send my partner.

6. the writing I send my partner will be returned to me; however, if a piece of writing is special, I should make a copy before I send it to my partner.
7. my signature on this form gives Candida Gillis, the project director, permission to quote from my writing in talks or articles about the project; I also understand that my full name will not be used and that my writing will be used only in a favorable context.
8. there are no guaranteed benefits from participating in this project.

PLEASE ANSWER:

What kinds of writing do you like to do (fiction, poems, essay, narrative, other)?

What do you like to write about?

Please provide the name and phone number of a character reference

Name:
Phone #:

Thank you!

Signature of community participant:
Date:

Print your name:
Phone #:
Address:

This contract has several key elements. The first item asks that the writer "communicate with [his or her] partner solely for the purpose of sharing and responding to writing." There are two reasons this item is included. First, Writing Partners is not a pen-pal program. The purpose is less to "get to know each other" (though obviously this does happen) than to learn about one's own and someone else's writing. Younger writers particularly can slip into the pen-pal mode, become more interested in chatting with their partners about their lives, and neglect to send writing. The second, related, reason is that the project is not an entree to a social relationship. I ask my college students not to send their e-mail addresses or to telephone, e-mail, or plan to meet their partners privately even if the younger writer asks. This restriction is for the protection of all concerned. In the past, some young partners have wanted to correspond with their older partners outside the project, and although these relationships might be innocent and friendly, the potential for problems exists. Of course, there is some flexibility here. Two writers sent writing through e-mail with the approval of the young partner's parents. Another community writer attended the same church as his partner and knew her family. But as a rule, I discourage contacts outside the writing exchange for the duration of the project in the same way, I am sure, that teachers whose students share writing through the Internet discourage personal meetings with correspondents and keep interchanges within school boundaries and monitored.

Items 4 and 5 address a similar issue. Teachers and administrators agreed at the outset that all writing should be sent through the teacher and/or project director. This policy enables the writing to be screened. Any time people outside school become involved with the school or with students, there is a need for some kind of safeguard; the young writers are minors and the school is responsible.

Engaging and Preparing Student Writers

Once writers in the community are interested in sharing writing, the task is to solicit interest from students. As I noted earlier, students who like to write and who are willing to share writing with a community writer come in all shapes and sizes, interests and abilities. Most need no encouragement to join the project once they realize that 1) they can send work in progress that does not have to be polished to perfection (in fact, students sometimes get more out of having a partner when they send writing they are clearly struggling with), 2) the purpose of the exchange is not tutorial, 3) they do not have to be Shakespeare or even on the staff of the literary magazine to participate, and 4) they may send a variety of writing, including writing done in class for assignments or writing done privately outside school. The single most important qualification for participation is the desire to do it. *Participation must be voluntary*. One teacher tried giving extra credit for having a partner but found that students who participated *only* for extra credit took their partnerships less seriously and wrote perfunctorily and less often. Commitment to writing is the central, most important requirement. Others are the ability to send new writing regularly and the willingness to read and respond thoughtfully and fully to the partner's writing. Although many of the students in our project are enrolled in creative writing classes or work on student publications, many are neither; they simply enjoy writing and may have more time to devote to their partners than students more involved in other activities.

The best time to generate enthusiasm for Writing Partners and to get students interested in having partners is at the beginning of the semester when the energy (yours and theirs) is high. In our project, the teachers begin the semester with a pep talk about the opportunities a partnership affords. (Because our project is established, many students already know about it and are eager to join.) Then they give packets of the following materials to students who express an interest: a letter for students explaining Writing Partners; a contract similar to the one for community writers ("Student Writing Partners' Responsibilities"); a letter to parents explaining the project attached to 1) a copy of the guidelines for selecting community writers and 2) a permission form for signature. Like the letter to community writers, the letter for students outlines the program and states what they can expect. All the responsibilities and procedures are explained in a general way.

Dear Student,

Do you like to write? Are you a poet, a writer of stories? Do you like to write memories, letters, essays? If so, you might like to participate in the Writing Partners Project. You don't need to be a "great" writer to join; all you need is to enjoy writing and sharing your work with another writer.

Writing Partners is a program that pairs writers in the schools with older writers in the Moscow community for the purpose of exchanging and responding to each others' writing. The aim of the project is to give younger writers wider audiences and support for their writing and to foster a larger community of writers—people of all ages who write for pleasure and who share common struggles and successes. Here is how the Writing Partners Project works:

If, after you have read this letter, you would like to have a writing partner, you should give the attached "Dear Parent or Guardian" letter and materials to your parent or legal guardian, have him or her sign the "Parent Permit" form, and return it to your English teacher. Also, you should sign and return to your teacher the "Student Writing Partners' Responsibilities" form that directly follows this letter. It is your contract for participation in the project. Once we receive the forms, your teacher and I will pair you with a community writer who has been selected to participate. Your partner will be either a student in a writing course at the University of Idaho or another adult in the Moscow community who has been chosen to participate in the program.

After your forms are turned in, you will receive a letter from your writing partner, along with some writing the partner wishes to share with you. The writing might be poetry, personal reminiscence, fiction, or essay, depending on the interests of the writer. You should respond with a short letter in which you introduce yourself, react to the writing your partner has sent, and send some writing of your own. (This is what makes Writing Partners different from pen pals; writing partners share their writing!) Include any questions you might want to ask your partner about your writing. The writing you send might be writing you have done for school (book responses, essays, poetry) or outside school. It may be writing in progress and in draft form, so long as it is legible (readers enjoy writing more if it is polished). Writing partners are not to be critics or editors or teachers. Instead, they should be interested, supportive readers. Your responses to your partner's writing and the ones you receive to your writing should be positive and constructive. Your participation in Writing Partners will not affect your school grade, and you may stop participating at any time. However, if you do agree to participate, please make a commitment to send writing regularly. Don't let your partner down.

For the duration of the project, you and your partner will exchange and respond to each other's writing regularly. *All writing and letters are to be exchanged through the teachers and me*. You will turn in all writing and letters for your partner to your English teacher; I will then make sure I get it from your teacher and take it to your partner. In the same way, I will give your teacher writing from your partner to go to you. You will not meet your partner until the end of the semester, and you should communicate with your partner for no purpose other than to share and respond to writing. I may read your and your partner's letters and writing to keep informed as to how the activity is going. Your partner may wish to share your writing with others; if you want your writing to be read by no one but me and your partner, you should let us know and we will respect your wishes. In addition, I may use parts of your writing and/ or letters to the partner in presentations or publications about the project. If so, I will use the writing only in a positive context and will not cite your full name. Your parent's or guardian's signature on the "Parent Permit" and your signature on the "Student Writing Partners' Responsibilities" form constitute permission for me to quote from your writing in presentations and/or publications about the project. If you want to participate in the project but do not want me to quote from your writing, please indicate this on the forms.

At the end of the project, the University of Idaho Writing Workshop for Teachers class will produce an anthology of writing submitted by students and their partners. The anthologies will be available at cost; there is no obligation to buy one. Also, you will be invited to a reception for all the writing partners at the end of the term to meet and celebrate your work. Your participation in the project officially ends at this time.

If you would like to have a writing partner, give the "Dear Parent or Guardian" letter and permit forms to your parent(s). Return the signed "Parent Permission" form to your English teacher, along with your signed "Student Writing Partners' Responsibilities" form. And start writing!

Sincerely,
Candida Gillis, Project Director
Department of English, University of Idaho

The student contract attached to this letter parallels the one for community writers. It explains, this time for the young writers, that the interaction between partners should be limited to the exchange of writing, and that their writing should be sent through and may be read by the teacher and me. We discovered that students, even more than community writers, need to have these points emphasized; Liza and Daniel (not their real names) are a case in point. Daniel was a college student assigned to Liza, a prolific writer in the ninth grade. Liza had several pen pals and wanted to write to Daniel at his home address. She asked Daniel to write to her directly, too, and not to send his writing through her teacher and me. Daniel was a prolific writer who turned out page after page of freewriting in the style of Kerouac, much of it on mature subjects. Daniel wanted some day to teach English but hated the authoritarian structure of the public schools and had many friends of high school age who visited him at home; in all innocence, he saw nothing amiss about being good friends with his students. He was not pleased that Liza's teacher and I discouraged him from developing a relationship with Liza outside what he perceived to be the restrictive environment of the project and the public school system. He complained in a letter to Liza that her teacher and I were censoring his work. (We were not; we were merely asking him to conform to the guidelines of the project.) It took many conferences to convince Daniel that the policy of sending writing through us might be in his and Liza's best interests. Liza's teacher also managed to convince Liza, and for the duration of the semester, the two corresponded more publicly. (After the semester, however, Daniel decided that he did not want to teach in public schools and dropped out of the teacher education program.) The "Student Writing Partners' Responsibilities" form, when signed and kept on file, is a good reminder to students who need it that the purpose of the project is to develop appreciation for and increase understanding of writing and writing processes.

STUDENT WRITING PARTNERS' RESPONSIBILITIES

Please read, sign, answer the questions on the bottom of the page and return to your English teacher along with your signed "Parent Permit" form.

As a participant in the Writing Partners Project, I promise that I will

1. send, through my teacher, some of my original writing to my partner at least every two weeks.
2. read my partner's writing and send written comments about his or her writing that are helpful and supportive.
3. return my partner's writing and comments in a timely fashion.
4. notify the project director immediately if I wish to discontinue the program.

I understand that

1. if I have problems with the program, I may freely share my concerns with the project director and my English teacher.
2. if I do not respond to and send writing regularly, I may be asked to discontinue the program.
3. all writing and letters to my partner will go through my teacher and the project director; likewise, all writing from my partner will come through the director and teacher; I will not send material to my partner in the mail or through e-mail.
4. my English teacher and the project director may read the writing I send my partner.
5. the writing I send my partner will be returned to me; however, if the writing is special, I should make a copy before I send it to my partner.
6. the project director may quote from my writing in talks or articles about the project according to the procedure described in the letter to parent or guardian.
7. the aim of the program is to help participants appreciate and enjoy writing, and my participation is voluntary.

PLEASE ANSWER:

What kinds of writing do you like to do (stories, poems, essay, narrative, other)?
What do you like to write about?
Signature of student participant:
Date:
Print your name:

Teachers have found that, by signing this contract, students are more inclined to take their responsibilities seriously. If they renege on their promises to respond "in a timely fashion" and to send writing regularly, they have broken their contracts; teachers are then free to ask them to quit the project and assign their partners to others more reliable.

Informing Parents

Having a writing partner as part of a school project requires full, informed consent of students' parents or guardians. Attached to each "Dear Student" letter and contract are materials for the student's parents: a letter containing essentially the same information as the student's letter, a permit form for them to sign and return (see Appendix), and a copy of the guidelines for selecting community writers. The letters for parents and students are nearly identical (the parent letter contains slightly more detail). Initially, I planned to use one letter for both to save paper but decided that parents merited letters of their own, so that they would feel "officially" informed and in case they had questions later on. After five years, I have not had one parent call with a question, so I assume my strategy is effective.

Securing Administrator Support

It should go without saying that a Writing Partners Project requires support from principals, department heads, and/or other appropriate school administrators. When my project was still just an idea, I talked to English department heads and building principals, who were extremely helpful and encouraged me to get the project underway. They were pleased that the university was interested in working with their schools and welcomed the involvement of the community. Because the project helps build stronger relations between school and community, enables students to learn more about writers and writing in the world outside school, and potentially showcases the work of students and teachers (a local newspaper article featured the reception and project), the administrators I work with are enthusiastic. Understandably concerned about careful selection of community writers and about the need to provide information to parents and to systematically organize and oversee the exchanges, administrators appreciate a project that has been carefully thought out and anticipates potential problems. A packet of all the materials given in this chapter can help secure their support.

As soon as administrators give their OK, the writers have been engaged, the parents notified, the signed forms returned, and the first "Dear Writing Partner" letters collected from community writers, the task is to pair writers and let the exchanges begin. So on to Chapter 3.

> Writing Partners is enrichment for the classroom teacher and for the student. It's sometimes work, an additional assignment, and additional responsibility, but a motivating one for the student who is interested in his writing and the writing of others. And it's an additional one to coordinate. But when the junior high and [community] writer-combination really cares about writing and reading and receiving, what a marriage!
>
> Susan Hodgin, Eighth-Grade English Teacher
> Moscow Junior High School

3

Off and Running

Dear Writing Partner,

Greetings from your University friend. My name is Saundra, and I am a junior at the University of Idaho. I also went to junior high in Moscow, so chances are I was once in the very same English class that you are in now.

I am looking forward to writing to you and exchanging writing samples. I have enclosed sort of a silly poem that I wrote in Sociology class the other day. I know I should have been paying attention to the teacher, but I was feeling sort of creative that day. A girl came into our class dressed in the most outrageous outfit that I have ever seen. I could not help but get out a piece of paper and write a poem about her. I hope you enjoy it.

I am trying to write other works to send to you. I usually write very little poetry (it is my worst!), and I am working on a short story right now. A lot of my writing is autobiographical—I like to write about my own personal experiences. I will try to send you as many different writing samples as I can.

I really am looking forward to writing to you and reading what you are working on. Thanks for being my Writing Partner.

Sincerely,
Saundra

Dear Writing Partner,

Hello and Howdy-Do! My name is Michael—I'm a student here at the University of Idaho, and also a hopeful writing partner-to-be. In my long and illustrious life (almost 23 years), I've done all kinds of writing: poetry, short stories, autobiographical, creative non-fiction, and even a few failed attempts at novels (I didn't know what I was getting myself into). I've found that writing is the perfect creative cure-all—no matter what kind of mood you're in, writing helps the hurt go away, or saves the fun for a rainy day. Sharing your experiences (which always sound more exciting once you've written about them) with others is one of the best reasons to write—and is also why I'm excited about this writing partners program. I've enclosed a short, semi-silly poem about a fall day, just to give you an idea of how I write. I certainly don't think it's award-winning material, but it's kind of fun. Write back soon!

Michael

Dear Writing Partner:

I'm looking forward to exchanging prose with you. I've found over the years that other people's suggestions, observations and input can help me improve my writing. So I'll appreciate whatever you have to say. Don't worry about whether I'll like your observations or whether I'll agree with your ideas.

I'm not telling you much about myself in this letter because the first piece I'm sending you covers that territory. It's an exercise I was asked to do for a job application. And I wonder how people react to it—what's missing, what could be left out, or whether it's complete.

What this essay doesn't tell you is that I free-lanced my first story in 1981 for $28 and a few cents. I am now senior reporter in the Pullman bureau of the *Moscow-Pullman Daily News* and I cover Washington State University and environmental issues.

I still free-lance whenever possible, for a variety of publications from newspapers to magazines. For some publications, the pay rate hasn't improved dramatically.

I look forward to hearing from you.

Sincerely,
Ken

The project is off and running when the community writers send their first letters to the young writers. As I explained in Chapter 2, I ask the community writers to begin the exchange by writing introductory "Dear Writing Partner" letters. Although one might begin the other way around, with students writing the introductory letters, the pairings seem to be more successful when community writers go first. The presence of actual letters in the classroom makes young writers eager to write back. And students who want a partner but are slow to return their signed forms get a real boost when they know partners letters are waiting for them.

Pairing writers can occur in several ways. In our project, the teachers match writers based on various factors, particularly their knowledge of their students' writing interests and abilities. Some factors that influence teachers' placements include whether a student has a preference for poetry or prose, whether a young writer might be inspired or inhibited by the quantity or complexity of the community writer's work, personal interests or backgrounds expressed by the writers, and sometimes gender. Susan Hodgin, the eighth-grade teacher quoted at the end of Chapter 2, uses two strategies to match partners:

> I call the first method "the grab bag approach." If all the students are new to me, I usually ask my participating students to come to the front of the class, forming a circle on the floor if numbers allow. Then I spread out the first letters—and my students read until they find a partner of choice; then I record the partners for my future roster. My students really enjoy this part, and they especially enjoy reading every letter if they're still in the circle. This process continues as I move through my scheduled day, which is usually a disadvantage for the afternoon students because the pickings are usually slim by then. (When Candy's students [my college partners] agree to write two—and sometimes three—partners I usually save the duplicate first letters for those afternoon students, so they can get some selection.)
>
> The second method of distribution becomes a little more subjective for me because I know my students better, and I know who will need a more conscientious partner, or which ones prefer a poet or a humorist, and so on. . . . Sometimes the pairing process becomes the best marketing for the program; other students become interested and want to participate as well. And some of these students often make some of the more faithful writing partners because they want to; it's not a course requirement.

Pairings are sometimes playful: Susan once paired a college student whose last name was Golightly with an eighth grader named Upthegrove. And students often pick partners with the same first name. Once writers are paired and the young writers know their partners' names and something about them, the exchange is underway. The teachers usually ask for a first response within one week; the quick turnaround weeds out the occasional student who thinks he wants to have a writing partner but isn't willing to produce writing. But most are eager to write back with their own introductory letters and writing:

> Dear Saundra,
>
> My name is Katie. I am a sophomore at Moscow High School. I am glad to be your writing partner. I have participated in this program once before, in 8th grade. I really enjoyed it, and I am looking forward to exchanging writing with you.
>
> I am enclosing two poems that I wrote this summer. I hope you don't have trouble reading them. I usually prefer to write my poems in my own hand-writing. I hope you like them and please tell me what you think of them.

I really liked your poem. I can relate to the poem because I have had people that had to go away. I think you wrote the poem beautifully.

Sincerely,
Katie

Dear Michael,

I think you have a really cool name—seeing as my name is Michael. I am a student at MJHS in the eighth grade. I hope to have a fun time in the writing partners program. In the past I have written short stories, a miserable autobiography—written in fifth grade—and especially poems. I have included a poem I wrote for English this year. We were supposed to write a poem about ourselves but I just sort of made it up and I went along. If you think it's morbid that's because it is.

I thought your Leaf Poem was extremely good especially the last line about the rake!

Michael

Dear Ken,

My name is Allen and I'm going to be your writing partner this year. I'm a sophomore at MHS, 16 years old on November 14. This is not my first experience with writing partners. I've exchanged writings with people twice before.

You're a reporter? I've often thought of being a reporter or publisher or something. As an 8th and 9th grader I was the editor-in-chief of the MJHS literary magazine *Ursa Major*. We won a couple of national awards and had a lot of fun doing it. [*Ursa Major* was the winner of Merlyn's Pen's 1994 Golden Pen Award and the 1993 Silver Pen Award.]

This week I'm sending a poem I wrote in English about the Internet. I wrote it because my teacher said that she didn't think I could write a good poem with meter and rhyme about something as unpoetic as the Internet.

I really liked your autobiography, especially the first line, "I'm the accidental journalist." It really set the tone for the whole piece.

Allen

Some young partners are more comfortable than others writing to a near-stranger. Angela, whose correspondence with another partner, Lindy, is included in Chapter 5, is chatty and at ease introducing herself to Russ:

Dear Russ,

My name is Angela and I am an 8th grader at the junior high.

I love to write, and I love reading pieces of work that have been (or are being) written by people that I know. . . so the writing partners project is a lot of fun for me.

Since I play volleyball in the fall, and during my off-season I'm a cheerleader—it's usually pretty hard for me to find time to write, but I definitely try.

Writing has been a major part of my life ever since I was five or six years old (my mom always made me make up stories and stuff). But even though it was "just another one of those things you have to do 'cause Mommy says so," when I was younger, now, I think of it in a considerably happier light (thank goodness).

Well, I'm really looking forward to getting to know you better (through your writing and your letters), and I just have a feeling that this is going to be a fun semester!

Angela

P. S. Your essay was great!! I have to admit that the length was a bit intimidating at first, but once I started reading it, that all stopped mattering.
Oh yeah, I like the title!

P. P. S. I almost forgot!. . . I enjoy writing everything from stories, to poems, to letters (usually having something to do with young urban youth).
Enclosed is one of my favorite pieces of mine, my latest poem.

Zac's and Chris' personalities are quite different and no less unique:

Dear Scott,

My name is Zac and I go to Moscow Junior High School. My favorite class is Creative Writing. I like to read and write too. I like to read poetry and write short stories. I want to become a book editor when I graduate from college. I'm looking forward to meeting you, and I liked your story. I thought it interesting about how he created a pen to hold info. . . . The story I have enclosed is one I route [sic] in the seventh grade. It's about a man who has writer's block. I would appreciate it if you would give me a response, and would you please tell me if I misspelled a word.

Dear Writing Partner:

My name is Chris, and when I send you different samples of my writing I was wondering if I could just start these little letters with your first name. I really don't know what a free-lance piece of writing is, maybe you could try to explain that to me, and I also write some poetry but I don't keep a journal other than the one I have located above my brain stem. I really did enjoy your writing that came with your letter, and I felt that you had given rather good detail in describing the alarm clock. Sometimes I have to arise to one of them my self.

Now the young writers wait for a response. Once they receive their second letter and writing from their partners, they should write back and send more writing within two weeks. It usually takes the community writer a week or two to write, so young writers have *at least* two weeks between their first letter and their next to accumulate more writing. Reading and responding to their partners' writing does not take long.

Keeping Track of the Exchanges

At this point, it is a good idea to make up a master list with partners' names, the classes they are in, and any necessary telephone numbers. I keep lists like this in strategic locations—a few at work, several at home, one by each phone. For my purposes, a list of partners broken down by school and teacher is the most helpful. I have experimented with a variety of structures, and here are several:

WRITING PARTNERS: FALL '95

Moscow Junior High
MRS. HODGIN (Phone #)

Student	Class/Period	College Writer Phone #
Joseph M.	(8–5)	Mark J.
Jon M.	(CW–8)	"
Kristen N.	(8–5)	Elizabeth M.
Adam J.	(CW-8)	"
		Community Writer Phone #
Amy P.	(8–5)	Ian A.
Nick L.	(CW–8)	José M.

In this format, young writers are listed on the left, their partners on the right (the college students generally have two partners each). In parentheses are the young writers' classes (8 means eighth-grade English, CW means Creative Writing). I find that grouping college and community writers separately simplifies the collection and distribution of writing. Another format I like places all partners on the left, the young partner on top, the community or college writer beneath (or the other way around):

MOSCOW SENIOR HIGH PARTNERS

Mrs. Hughes (phone #)

Camas G.
Elsie M. (C) (phone#)

Katie R.
Saundra W. (309) (phone #)

Mrs. Wear (phone #)

Dianna G.
Karen H. (401) (phone #)

Roshan K.
Phil D.(C) (phone #)

In this format, the letter or number in parentheses indicates the "home base" of writers: C means community at large; a number indicates that the writer is a college student enrolled in an English department writing course designated by the number. College students and community writers are not separated, although I have made similar lists that grouped partners by the home base of the senior writer. By keeping all the names on the left, I am able to use the space on the right to record the dates when a partner has received or sent writing. Sometimes I put columns to the right (S for date sent, R for date received):

S R S R S R S R

Community Writers:

Phil M. (phone #)
Susan G. (MHS, Mrs. C.)

Ron M. (phone #)
Joe G. (MJHS, Mrs. H.)

College Writers:

English 401:

Mike R. (phone #)
Sally P. (MHS, Mrs. G)
Rhonda F. (MJHS, Mr. Q.)

In this example, the senior writers are listed first, and the abbreviations in parentheses indicate the school and teacher. For her own record-keeping, one teacher prefers a master list by period, shown in Figure 3-1.

It is important to keep track of when writers write their partners. Students often cannot remember when they have last sent writing; sometimes they think they are owed writing from their partners when, in fact, it is they who owe. Record-keeping can be confusing without some kind of master list. Susan generally has over thirty writing partners spread over eight periods in any given semester. When her students send letters, she checks their names off on her master list and notes the date, so she knows that those students expect to receive writing. Another teacher posted a master list next to a collection envelope so students themselves could record the dates they sent writing.

FIGURE 3–1

Writing Partners

Class	MJHS W.P.		U.I. W.P.
CW-8	Mary	and	Cheryl
CW-8	Trent	and	David
CW-8	Nicolet	and	Anne Marie
CW-8	Avery	and	Suzanne
CW-8	Matthew	and	Gary
CW-8	Diane	and	Shauna
CW-8	Tammy	and	Matt
CW-8	Shayla	and	Anne Marie
CW-8	Annie	and	Jodi
CW-8	Josh	and	Kristen
CW-8	David	and	Phil
CW-8	Nate	and	Sandy
CW-8	Tiffany	and	Teah
CW-8	Matt	and	Jodi
CW-8	Brittany	and	Sara
CW-8	Scott	and	Dave
7-__	Adam	and	David
9-4	Adrienne	and	Ralph
9-5	Kym	and	Krystle
9-5	Andrea	and	Stephanie
9-5	Hannah	and	Timothy

Writing Partners' Reception is at MJHS's Library on Tuesday, May 7th from 7-9 p.m.

The Messenger Service

I have found no ideal way to pick up and deliver writing to partners, though over the years I have learned a few shortcuts. Because our town is small, I can easily drive by each participating school at least once a week and pick up and deliver writing. I also have bribed my son, a high school student, to be my messenger service. Usually, the teachers leave the writing they have collected from their students in an envelope either in the school office or in another strategic location (taped to their door, sitting in the chalk well) for me to pick up, and I deliver writing for the partners to the teacher's classrooms or school mailboxes. One teacher created specially marked "For Writing Partners" and "From Writing Partners" envelopes and stapled them to the bulletin board. The envelopes are convenient drop-off and pick-up places, preventing the writing partners' letters and writing from getting mixed up with class assignments and other work on the teacher's desk. The students are always anxious to look inside the envelopes and are reminded to write. This system also cuts down on the time needed to pass out and collect letters.

In terms of getting writing to and from the community writers, the postal service is the easiest, despite the expenses of postage and envelopes (I always include a self-addressed, stamped envelope to make it easier for a writer to send work back), and the inconvenience of addressing envelopes (although student partners can do this). Printed mailing labels, including self-addressed, are a help.

Because I work at the university, exchanges between the young writers and their college partners are not difficult. I take the letters to my class and distribute them to my students. During semesters when some college partners are not enrolled in my class, the exchange is trickier. I first tried a system of putting writing in the mailboxes of faculty in whose courses the partners were enrolled, but the procedure depended on reliable instructors with the time and memory to deliver the material to their students and on students who regularly attended class. Like the teacher with the bulletin board, I devised a more efficient system of "To" and "From" envelopes attached to my office door, one for dropping off and one for picking up writing. This system does require that partners develop the habit of checking the envelopes weekly and that occasionally I call a partner whose writing is overdue, but overall, the system is far easier than any other, with the exception of having all college partners concentrated in one college class. I highly recommend this strategy for a teacher in junior or senior high school who is running the project. A packet of letters can be mailed every two weeks, or delivered in person if the college is not too far away. Many teachers of college writing and/or education courses are eager to work with teachers in local schools and serve as liaisons, not only helping teachers locate college writers but also taking charge of the distribution and pick-up of writing. Providing that the instructors are like-minded and agree on the purposes of a Writing Partners Project, securing their cooperation should not be difficult.

When to Write

At one time, the teachers and I experimented with a calendar of due dates so the writers knew exactly when they had to have writing to send their partners. This system sounded good in theory, but it never worked practically. Students are sometimes absent and miss their dates, so the schedule was always changed. Community (including college) writers do not send their responses back at the same time if they use the mail or a drop-off envelope;

some are quicker than others to respond to their partners. College instructors can more easily set deadlines for the writers in their classes, but even these deadlines fall apart when students are absent. In addition, writers tend to work on different deadlines and have different motivational levels. Susan Hodgin observes:

> The intended schedule for partners is every two weeks, but if a student misses class, then the writing exchange schedule gets off. Again, the more conscientious student usually gets back on track pretty quickly, but some students just don't. These same students don't get as much from their semester because their exchange lacks the frequency of some of the other partners.
>
> Some of the writing partners are what I nickname "natural writers." Such students don't wait for a teacher assignment to write. For them, writing has become their passion or their hobby. These are the writers that I think most profit from Writing Partners. These students don't have deadlines for a final draft. When they actually send their writing to their partner, their writing is still in process—or they're often earnestly seeking some feedback, and so the two-week turnaround period for letters and writing is no problem for them.
>
> On the other hand, some junior high partners who enjoy writing are overcommitted, and all they have time to write are their classroom assigned writings. For these students, the two-week turnaround may be too late for feedback for assigned writings. The conscientious student will work hard and independently, without his partner's feedback—and then send a copy of the finished work and expect a figurative pat on the back, which he will usually get in a comment like "Nice job. I enjoyed your writing. You made me remember the time I once. . . ." The weaker student writer may still benefit from the exchange, but the turnaround time may not benefit his grade, which he actually wanted on the assignment.

When Writers are Late

As Susan describes, every so often young writers get behind in responding to their partners often for legitimate reasons, and need a little push back on track:

> I've decided to try my hand at typing a letter seeing as how I'm really tired and my brain is broken because I had to write a four page long report for biology. . . .
>
> The piece (if you could call it that) that I have sent you this time is really a brain storm which I had to start getting on paper. Unfortunately I haven't had much time to write with all my activities. Track just started at school. I have to preside over Technology Club on Thursdays and Odyssey of the Mind occupies my weekends. Not to mention saxophone

lessons and school work. But the way I look at it is if you don't keep busy you get bored!

I'm sorry I won't be much help this time, one of my friends and his father, who I also knew, died yesterday. . . .

Trying to keep track of over thirty writers and their various two-week limits is a headache, so we leave it to the writers to set their own schedules and remind them if they seem to fall way behind. A sign taped to the wall in a visible place is a good reminder (Figure 3-2).

Sometimes I use form notes if a writer is long overdue:

Dear _____

Your writing partner has not heard from you in a while! Please send writing as soon as you can; he or she is anxious to hear from you. If you

FIGURE 3–2

HAVE YOU
WRITTEN
YOUR
WRITING
PARTNER
LATELY?

are having trouble responding to your partner's writing or wish to drop out of the Writing Partners program, please let your teacher know.

Thanks, and keep writing!

Another effective method is for the senior writer to write her tardy partner a "where are you?" note. These usually produce results, though sometimes it takes more than one note to jar loose a busy ninth grader, and the notes are an added burden for the community writer. Post-it notes on a bulletin board, lists of "People Who Owe Writing" on a blackboard, short conferences, and at-home phone calls from the teacher or from me are also effective. If a young writer does not write despite reminders, the teacher may ask him or her to discontinue the project. Because so many students want partners, we generally have a waiting list, so if a writer is asked to quit the program, another is ready and eager to step in.

If a community writer falls behind (which also happens rarely), I phone or send a personal note. While I do not want to nag people and make them regret their participation in the project, I also know how discouraged young writers become if they do not hear back promptly from their partners. Looking in the "From" envelope and finding nothing is as disappointing as no mail at camp.

"What Do I Say to My Partner?"

As I noted in Chapter 2, writers in the community who have not worked with young writers may want guidance in responding to their partners' work. Because the project de-emphasizes editing and focuses more on encouraging, supporting, and mentoring, writers are sometimes uncertain as to how to do this in a way that will be genuinely helpful for their partners. Young writers, too, may be unsure of how to respond, especially to work that is "over their heads" or "different" from the writing of their peers that they are used to reading and critiquing. To help educate community writers without giving them a whole course in writing pedagogy, I developed a list of suggestions for responding to partners' writing. I intended the list to be practical, give specific suggestions for responding, and cover all eventualities without appearing prohibitively detailed or complex. You will note that the audience for these suggestions is people who are not professional educators. I tried to avoid jargon and to give examples wherever possible.

SUGGESTIONS FOR RESPONDING TO YOUR PARTNER'S WRITING

1. *Respond as a supportive fellow writer*, not as a teacher or authority figure. You can do this by avoiding judgmental words such as "good," or "excellent."

2. *Give your partner your reactions.* You might mention

  - how the piece made you feel (made you laugh, feel sad, etc.).
  - what it reminded you of in your own experiences.
  - what it made you see, hear, think about.

3. *Tell what you liked* about the piece—a particular part that stood out for you (a phrase, section of dialogue, a description, a character) and why. Again, avoid judgmental words. Better to say "I liked the description of ____" than "the description of ____ was good."

4. *If your partner has asked a question, answer it.* If your partner has asked for criticism, give it, but be positive. Sometimes people ask for criticism but aren't ready to be shot with both barrels (few of us are). If your partner has asked "how do you like it?" a good strategy is to tell how it made you feel and what you liked about it; explain some specific features you especially liked. If you didn't like the piece, try to find something in it you *did* like (the subject, the attempt to capture an event or mood, the experimentation with dialogue, the action, etc.), and then explain what didn't work for you: "I wanted to know more about ____," "I got confused toward the end because ____," or "I liked the parts best where you didn't tell me what you were feeling but let me infer your feeling through the description."

5. *Be honest without being cruel or gushy.* "Excellent!" doesn't tell the writer much (besides, it's judgmental). Many young writers hear lots of praise from their families and friends and welcome positive, constructive suggestions. Here are some examples:

Question: "Do you like the title?"

Positive response: "It doesn't seem to fit this poem. It makes me think of something else. How about ____?"

(Avoid negative responses: "Not really; it's off the subject.")

Question: "Was my story exciting?"

Positive responses: "The first part got my attention right away. In the middle I got confused because I didn't know who all the new characters were. This distracted me and I lost the suspense. Could you bring the characters in the beginning, so I could focus on the action?" Or "The story itself is very exciting. It would be more exciting, though, if you cut down on the description. I found myself wanting to know what happens next but I had to read through some description to get to it. The description is interesting and vivid, but for me, it got in the way of the action."

(Avoid negative responses: "Not really. You had too much description and not enough action.")

Be careful of sarcasm. It might be taken the wrong way and be hurtful.

6. *Be sparing* in your answers to your partner's questions. The writer may want to know "how did you like it?" in a few sentences, not a full-page lecture. However, some writers want more criticism or advice than others and you'll need to judge what your partner wishes. Consider his or her age and writing ability. In general, one or two suggestions is sufficient. If you give too many you may overwhelm and intimidate your partner. However, you want to give enough of a response to be helpful.
7. *Be encouraging.* Phrases such as "I'd love to hear more about ____ " or "I'm dying to know what your character looks like" can make the writer feel rewarded and motivated at the same time.
8. *Be enthusiastic* about the features of the writing you liked. If a piece moved you, touched you, affected you strongly, let the writer know. Evoking real feeling is a sign of powerful writing.

Thank you again for being a partner! If you have concerns or questions about your partner's writing or how to respond, don't hesitate to give me a call!

Candida Gillis
Writing Partners Project Director

One of the most important characteristics of feedback that writers seem to want is honesty. Often young writers feel that others praise their work without giving them helpful criticism. I have read this sentiment expressed in various ways by young writers:

Dear Kate,

My name is Crystal but I prefer to be called Livada. I am an eighth grader. My favorite subject right now is chorus. I hope to be a surgeon or singer when I become older. . . . I don't write very well, but I do read a lot. At least a half a book a day. So far I've found I like all types of writing except Romance. Yes, I do like Autumn, but I think Spring is my favorite season. The snow melting and all the crocuses, daffodils, and tulips push their way through the ground to the light. Then everything bursting into color. There are some poems on the next page that I thought up earlier today. They may be a bit sad but I was a bit depressed when I wrote them. Could you tell me, honestly, what you think of them? I'm tired of false answers from friends.

Livada's feelings are typical, especially for writers who are used to receiving high grades in English and/or praise from friends who are not writers themselves. Adolescents can be understandably mistrustful of empty flattery and want their partners to treat them as *real* writers, capable of growth, and mature enough to receive constructive criticism.

I hope you give me your honest opinion of [my poem] and I hope you like reading it.

I do need to develop [my story] more! But other than that do you like it? What should I do to improve it? *Remember, be truthful.*

I hope you will respond to my poem truthfully and honestly.

Like the rest of us, novice writers are understandably nervous about letting others see their writing. Adrienne expresses her uncertainties this way:

I am fourteen years old, I like to write poetry. I don't write much rhyme or humor because I don't have a knack for it, it ends up sounding forced. I don't have very many poems yet but I hope to have a large collection someday. Writing partners will hopefully help me with this.

This is my first year doing writing partners. I have to admit, I'm a little nervous about letting someone I hardly know read my writing. I am excited to get to know you and hope this year will be a good one!

To help young writers feel more comfortable sharing with partners and to encourage relationships of trust, I stress the necessity of responding in detail, avoiding the hollow, judgmental phrases like "good" or "wonderful!" and being positive. When readers explain their reactions in depth, writers tend to feel that their writing has been taken seriously and read with understanding and care. Thus, writers grow to be confident with each other and respect their partners' views. Michael's response to his junior partner's poem is specific and thoughtful:

I thought the poem you sent last week contained a lot of powerful imagery—the second stanza especially. Your lines about feeling "the death of the world upon my back" and "I worry that the disaster is me" really hit home with me. It made me remember that I'm not too far removed from your generation, and that the problems you'll face will be there waiting for me, too. Sometimes it's easy for us to think they'll go away, or that they aren't real—but turning your back won't keep them from biting you. Your poem certainly addresses these concerns and made me think about what I would do to face them.

In a similar vein, Ken, the journalist, gives Allen explicit feedback. Although he uses some judgmental terms, he backs up his evaluations with instructive and constructive observations:

Great stuff in your short story. The imagery was compelling. For example "every few hours, it seemed, the glass would glint fiendishly as its revolutions brought the sun into alignment." I also was taken by the way you described the shards of glass casting "tiny rainbows all about."

I remembered my own mishaps with glass objects. None of them ended so artfully.

It's well written, succinct and loaded with impact. You might consider whether the impact would increase if you skipped the one-sentence questions. . . for example, "what" and "what now." I also loved the detail about the fight with your brother and wouldn't have been turned away by more of that kind of detail.

Ken gives useful advice without sounding unduly critical or harsh.

Young writers also need suggestions for how to respond to their older partners' writing. Many tend to dismiss the writing with "great," or "I loved it," offering no detail or help. If the partners are to be genuine co-writers, both have the same responsibility to read and reflect on their partner's writing with care. When young writers are busy with other projects, they may not take the time that they should to respond in detail. One teacher in our project remedied this by insisting that his students write their partners a response including a minimum of 1) how they liked the writing, 2) one specific thing they liked about it, and 3) one suggestion for change. This technique produced more thoughtful responses:

> Your story is MORBID! (No offense) But! It was very good. At first I felt sorry for Jeremy, Ha! I learned my lesson! I did have one question, was Jeremy dreaming this story in bed, or did he actually do it then go to bed and dream?

> Thanks for writing! I like your short story. It was great and very descriptive. One thing I found out was that if you don't read it carefully it doesn't make sense. But I read it word by word and it was superb for a short story, and had good vocabulary. That was really neat about your relatives.

> I liked your story a lot. Eliot reminds me of a friend of mine. Your descriptions of him were very, very good. I was able to picture him coloring the sky puce. The picture you guys colored must be very lovely. You described it so well that I felt like I was actually sitting there watching you guys.

Although these writers do not give extensive suggestions for change, they do explain what they like or find confusing about the writing and how the writing affects them. Occasionally, however, a young writer goes into depth, as Lincoln does here:

> I really enjoyed your poem. I like the way it is so concise and swift in what it is saying. . . . I think this poem shows some father's quickness to react to "show how it's done." Sometimes this takes place without thinking whether it is right or not. Also I think that the father in this

poem is being very hard on himself (I'm reading a public speaking and leadership book and it talks a lot about self esteem) and this is portrayed very well. I felt bad for him and was glad not to be in his situation. One question I have though is: how do you decide where to break your line in your poems? It is a downright mystery to me because some are long and some are merely a word put there for no reason apparent to me.

Teachers can help students learn to respond productively by modeling, by providing rubrics, by encouraging partners to give the same quantity and quality of feedback they give each other in a workshop, and by occasionally providing class time for response. If teachers have their own partners, too, they can share their own responses and demonstrate the depth and range of comments that partners might appreciate.

Troubleshooting

Although, for the most part, the interchanges run smoothly, the project is not without its glitches.

Mismatched Partners

Every now and then, writers find they are not suited. For example, recently one ninth grader who considered herself a strong, serious writer of poetry was paired with a college student, an older woman returning to school, who also wrote much poetry. The college student enjoyed experimenting with voice and form, and her extensive portfolio included playful rhymes about everyday events in addition to free verse and more complex, highly personal poetry. Not certain of her younger partner's predilections, she initially sent a poem about a family pet. The young partner thought the poem was "too childish," and despite her teacher's counsel to send the older partner her own work and a letter explaining her preference in poetry, the girl did not want to continue the exchange. The teacher assigned a new partner to the college woman, and the younger student, who had been in Writing Partners the preceding semester, decided to drop out and devote her time to other activities.

On another occasion, one young writer simply did not understand her partner's writing. In response to her partner's question about whether she liked the poem she had sent, this eighth grader wrote candidly "I didn't like it. I don't like poetry." The older partner, who had no writing to share but poetry, made an effort to explain her work. The young partner, too, made an effort to appreciate it, but never gave much in the way of response. But because she liked her partner's letters, at least she stuck with the partnership. The teachers are careful, now, to warn their students that they may not like everything their partners write, and that they should ask questions when they do not understand, read with open minds, and seize the opportunity to learn about new forms of writing.

The Overzealous Responder

Despite my "best laid plans"—the suggestions for responding—a senior partner can take it upon himself or herself to be an editor or tutor. In the best case, the tutorial role is performed with sensitivity and is welcomed and appreciated by the young partner. In the worst case, which I have not experienced, the senior partner corrects, edits, and in other ways appropriates the writer's work to the discouragement of the young partner. One partnership was in between but came perilously close to the worst. The older partner was a student of creative writing. The younger partner, an eighth grader, was also a serious writer—on the staffs of the literary magazine and newspaper—who welcomed criticism; but he was used to workshop classes and taking responsibility for his own development as a writer. He was surprised when his older partner returned his short story with editorial comments penciled in on nearly every line: "This is repetitive. I will talk to you about this in my letter. It will be the first thing we work on, okay?" According to his teacher, the young writer wasn't sure how to take the plethora of advice that included suggestions for different words, phrases crossed out, words circled, and arrows everywhere amid exhuberant and mildly judgemental praise ("great detail," "vivid," "great vocabulary," "great metaphor"—the older partner, too, suffered from a tendency to repetition). Fortunately, the young man took the advice with good humor and as well-intended; a less confident writer might have felt discouraged or defeated. This episode taught me the importance of stressing in my initial conversations with prospective community writers that their role is not to edit and to be judicious in giving advice and not to mark on their partners' texts unless given permisson by the writer.

Inappropriate Writing

The topic of appropriateness is difficult because the definition of "appropriate" varies from writer to writer and from school to school. Our community is rural and agricultural yet includes a research university; parents hold a range of political and philosophical viewpoints and come from a variety of socioeconomic and ethnic backgrounds. A proportionately high number of students enter college or university. What may be acceptable to one child may offend another, although the public schools have experienced few censorship challenges.

In the five years that I have run Writing Partners, I have experienced only a few incidents of a young writer or parent objecting to a partner's writing and no community writer has complained. Occasionally, I have had to ask college partners not to send work that contains potentially offensive language or is about sensitive subjects (sex, drugs, violence) that, although acceptable in a college creative writing class, might seem out of place in a junior high (or even senior high) class. Younger teens tend to view college students as adults, almost like their teachers, and some can be shocked if their partners' writing contains language they may use themselves or tolerate from their peers. It may be easy for older writers unfamiliar with young adults and their expectations and experiences to overestimate the sophistication and reading maturity of their young partners. One college student majoring in creative writing sent his partner a parody of his fellow students' attempts at postmodern fiction. His partner was a very mature ninth grader, who would, so my student thought, appreciate the story's satirical exaggeration of the seamy, urban landscape. Alas, despite his exceptional fluency as a writer, the partner missed the satirical intent entirely and felt that the opening scene of a drunk man urinating in an alley was, in his words to his teacher, "inappropriate." When I talk to community writers, I make it a point to explain that if they are in doubt about the content or language of a piece, ask me or leave it out; a useful, general rule is to err on the side of conservatism.

Only once has a parent objected to the writing her child received. She was concerned because she felt this poem had sexual overtones:

GIVING IN

Only this: a scoured white bathtub freestanding
in a well-lit room with no curtains
that overlooks a careful garden gone
six days without a gardener.

The French doors are open
and I am bringing in pail after pail of walnut sized blackberries
to bathe in.

The purple rapture of their skin
on my skin dyes me dark as indigo,
dark as a blue bruise,
sweet as a dark night.

The light has failed, I cannot see
the porcelain, I have given in
to blackberry love.

Kenneth White

In discussions with the parent, Susan, the child's teacher, made the distinction between *sensual* and sexual and praised the poem for its use of sensual imagery. The parent seemed to understand and made no further complaint.

Personal Crises

Although Writing Partners' exchanges are supposed to be limited in focus to discussion of writing products and processes, many partners enjoy sharing events in their lives, their thoughts and feelings.

> So guess what. Tom moved Friday morning. I was so upset. Tuesday I had a basketball game and he was supposed to be there but he came late. So at half-time we came running out of the locker room and I had a big package with bows and ribbon. I threw it to him in the crowd. And I'll never forget the smile on his face. I give him a big Teddy bear. I'm going to miss him so much!

> I hope you had a great Valentine's Day weekend. I stayed at my dad's house for the weekend. I got to see my sister and my cat. On the way back it was really snowy and we almost got stuck!

Now and then a young partner will share painful and intimate information: a mother's death, a friend's suicide, a deadly automobile accident, a divorce, or the less tragic but certainly hurtful loss of a best friend or end of a romantic relationship. Because the exchanges are in a way public, shared with me and the young partners' teachers, the teachers and I become aware of these unhappy situations. (In our state, teachers are required by law to notify administrators if students write that they are victims of abuse or are considering hurting themselves or others.) Partners sometimes experience personal problems that interfere with their ability to write and to send writing to their partners, and I have on several occasions talked to a teacher about a partner's letters and have shared advice with my college students on how to respond. One sixth-grade girl, whom I will call Nina, was enthusiastic about the project at its outset and sent this letter of introduction along with several poems:

> Dear Partner,

> I'm very excited about this project. I think I'll like this. I'm getting a full set of braces on the 2nd of February. I am pretty scared. . . . I enjoy baby-sitting because I love kids. I would like to be a teacher and a writer when I'm old enough.

Soon into the semester, Nina stopped sending writing and began to tell her troubles to her partner. She wrote, "I like to write about my life because of the following: I like to write my feelings on paper. I have a lot of hard and horrible things I'm going through at the moment. . . . You may not enjoy this, but I feel like I should tell you before you learn more about me." She then told her partner about the murder of a close family member and other painful events in her recent life: "My heart will never be the same, it has torn half of my heart away." Her college partner was a sensitive woman with a great deal of experience working with adolescents. She responded supportively, gently turning the focus of the exchange back to writing:

> You know what? I think you are a wonderful writer and you are lucky to have the ability to write your feelings down on paper and be so expressive. Sometimes, I find, writing helps me sort out and think through my thoughts. I encourage you to continue writing. You're lucky as some people never find their niche in writing. You obviously have. And, thank you for your trust in me with all of your feelings and thoughts.
>
> I often write about my life (mostly growing up) and my family and all the memories I have. These things are a lot easier to write about than fiction.

In her next two letters, Nina sent little writing, instead reiterating the tragedy and her feelings. In speaking with Nina's teacher, I learned that Nina had a loving, supportive family and was getting along well in school. Nina's partner continued to send positive letters and writing that was upbeat, cheerful. By the end of the semester, Nina's letters were far happier, filled with chat about baseball and ballet, upcoming trips, and questions for her partner ("has anyone ever asked you to marry him?"), and she included some new poetry. Nina also had some words of gratitude for her partner:

> You have kept me company by your friendly letters and beautifully written stories and poems. Thanks a lot. Ever since _____ died I have felt kind of lonely in my heart. . . . At night I talk to him as if nothing happened and he was right there, but it helps a little to just talk to him. And you also helped me a lot. I thank you so much. I don't like to think of people as evil people, because we are all human beings and no one should be cruel to another. What do you think? I've had a lot of fun writing to you. I've really begun to think about writing books for people my age to read, if they like scary, freaky books like I do. Geez, I wrote a lot. I have never written a letter this long!

While Nina expressed her feelings in her letters, other young writers write out their feelings through poetry or essay.

PAIN

Rising, Swelling, Exploding, Fighting,
I don't want to let it free.
Ugly, Horrifying, Scary, Mean,
This is my secret.

Pushing, Shoving, Concealing, Blocking,
I don't want to share it.
Brave, Bold Strong, Able.
I'm fine on my own.
Weak, Scared, Blank, Alone,
This is what I am.
Nosy, Pushy, Curious, Inquisitive,
People try to help me.
Kind, Thoughtful, Wise, Loving,
She's falling away.
No one, Nobody, Gone, Invisible,
Everyone is gone.
Unloving, Uncaring, Unkind, Awful,
I pushed everyone away.
Empty, Cold, Shaky, Blind,
I feel all of this, I wish I didn't.

Nicole

An eighth grader's suicide prompted this poem by his friend, Meghan:

In Memory of My Friend

Fly free, little bird
Up, up, and away.
Fly free, little bird
I know you can't stay.

I fixed your wing
As best I could.
I helped you when
No one else would.

I've given you everything,
My heart and my soul,
And through this ordeal
I hope that you know

I've gone through a lot,
Such hurt and such pain,
Although you are gone
I love you just the same.

Fly free, little bird
Up, up, and away.
Fly free, little bird,
I know you can't stay.

The advice I give for writers whose partners share personal tragedies is to be supportive and sympathetic, but to steer the focus back to writing and the writing exchange, as Nina's partner did. And perhaps share and illustrate some ways their own writing has grown out of or even been shaped or enhanced by difficult events. ("Here is a poem I wrote about my own grandfather after his death. . . .") If the writing shows the positive that can come from sorrow, if it acknowledges sadness honestly but avoids dwelling in despair, the older partner can help the younger partner productively channel grief into writing. Russ inadvertently helped his younger partner, Angela, in this way when he sent her a poem about a loss in his life:

Russ,

Thanks for sharing your latest poem with me. . . another good one! But I'd have to say that "A Time to Grieve" is definitely my favorite so far. I really got a clear, bright, and vivid picture of the story (especially in the first five stanzas) with the hot air, bright sky, etc. . . . a picture-perfect moment slashed in half by tragedy.

I just happened to read "A Time to Grieve" for the first time on Monday of this week—the same day that I found out that two people who were really close to me had been killed. Though I had read your letter earlier, I still hadn't had a chance to look at the poem. So when I was flipping through my English folder, and came across it, the first stanza just hit me like a ton of bricks:

We all need the time
The time to grieve.
I try, but can't remember moments
We shared, you and I.

Just then, I realized that I needed to focus on the good things that we had all done together, instead of running through those million and one "what if" questions through my mind. Even though I still haven't been able to get myself to completely put my feelings on paper, your poem really helped me dig myself out of my little "hole." Muchas gracias.

Angela

One community writer who heard the writing partners read their work at our end-of-semester reception (described in Chapter 4), remarked that young people seem to write about such gloomy, depressing topics. But life is not always easy for teens (or anyone), many of whom must deal with complicated and difficult problems; adolescents' writing generally reflects the complexity of their age and the worlds they live in. I believe that those who can transform their problems into art that they share are strong, courageous, and healthy. I am heartened that writing is so valued, so useful, and so embraced by young people today. For every pain a partner writes about there is a joy, a bit of humor or silliness, an adventure, a moment of delight, a discovery. Young peoples' writing is, above all, vital.

FIGURE 3–3a

FIGURE 3–3b

FIGURE 3–3c

4

Celebrations

The culmination of our project is an anthology of partners' writing and a reception where writers come together to meet and read aloud samples of their work. Publishing is a final phase of the writing process, and an anthology enables the writing partners to cull from their semester's writing one or more pieces they would most like to include. The reception is a chance to celebrate, as a community, our love of writing and to appreciate the gifts of writing others give us.

The Anthologies

The logistics of putting together an anthology are not difficult but require careful organization. In our project, the anthologies are produced by the college students in my Writing Workshop for Teachers class. The younger writers and community writers send their material to us, and my students type, proofread, and lay out the book. The reason I put my students and not the students in the schools in charge of the production is that my students will be teachers soon, and they need experience with classroom publishing. Using desktop publishing software I bought with a small grant several years ago, I help my students learn, if they do not know already, how to import text, do layout, and add borders, shading, and graphics. In addition, my students learn the kinds of decisions involved in such a venture and some of the pitfalls of producing an attractive publication on a very small budget in a short period of time.

The first step in our production process is to solicit submissions from all partners. Two to three weeks before the end of the semester, I send announcements to every partner with deadlines for submission. (I've found it useful to make the deadline a few days earlier than absolutely necessary in case a writer is absent.) The announcement includes certain restrictions and

FIGURE 4–1

ATTENTION WRITING PARTNERS

THE ANTHOLOGY IS COMING!

Yes, we will once again publish an anthology of writing partners' astounding, amazing, amusing, and entertaining work. But we need your submissions. Get your material (no more than the equivalent of one, single-spaced page) to Mrs. Hodgin no later than Monday, April 22. Mark your submission "for the anthology." You do not need to type it; your partner will do that. Feel free to add illustrations, but make sure they are dark enough to be photocopied and can be cut and pasted to the typed copy.

Remember, your writing partner may not have copies of your writing. If you want something in the anthology, send it in again.

In early May we will let you know how much the anthologies cost and take orders. We will distribute the anthologies when we get together on Tuesday, May 7.

directions. First, we limit writers as to the amount they can submit. Because we sell the anthologies "at cost" to all the writing partners, we must keep them affordable by limiting each writer's number of pages. For a book of about twenty-five, two-sided pages, copying runs about $3.25 per book if we use less expensive bindings, paper, and card stock for covers, and no color reproductions. The amount a writer can send varies with the number of partners in the project. With sixty writers, we limit each to one, single-spaced page; if fewer, we set the limit at two pages. Because some writers submit

FIGURE 4–2

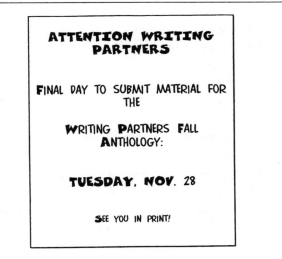

considerably less (one short poem for example), the teachers and I agree that an occasional longer work is fine. Second, we ask that any illustrations be dark enough to facilitate photocopying. Third, we inform writers that we will retype their work. By doing our own typing, we can control the type size and font, the spacing, and the arrangement. Although there are advantages in having the younger writers produce their own camera-ready copy, a more uniform anthology is generally better looking; and when writers are in different classrooms and even in different schools, as they often are in our project, uniformity is impossible. In addition, my students gain practice at copyediting.

Once we receive all the submissions, each college writer prepares the camera-ready pages containing her own, her partner's, and one community writer's submissions. She may add illustrations and must make the text error-free (the hardest job of all). As a class we decide what fonts we will use, working on the assumption that the anthology will look more professional with no more than two fonts, preferably one (and one should be an easy-to-read and widely available font such as Times New Roman, Palatino, or New Century Schoolbook). We also aim for a uniform type size and margins, although some students usually forget, and we end up reducing pages to accommodate the binding and make the text on the pages look more uniform. (In the past, I let everyone choose his own fonts and sizes, but the anthologies looked a bit chaotic. I also tried having each college partner put the material on a master disk for the editors, who had the job of producing the entire anthology. But as the project and the number of writers grew, the task became too big; I changed the system after one, thirty-hour weekend when my good-hearted volunteer editors nearly mutinied.) Having each college partner produce two to four polished pages seems to work pretty well, though the process is not perfect.

My students learn a great deal, not the least of which is how many ways there are to reproduce text. Some become highly creative and use the technology available at the university (the scanner, art files, various graphics) to enhance their pages. Others, for whom desktop publishing software is too confusing, intimidating, or inaccessible, make do with word processing software, simple cutting and pasting, and photocopying on acetate. (For the cover of *Rustlings of Thought*, shown in Figure 4-3, the text lines were photocopied onto acetates and laid over a copy of a picture.)

Another decision my students face is how much to change or edit their partners' work. My guideline is that editors should not change wording or basic structure and should keep all changes minimal so as to preserve the integrity, flavor, and voice of each piece. Spelling and punctuation errors should be corrected unless the usages are clearly intentional, as when a writer consistently avoids capitals or does not punctuate a poem. However, if the writer has changed tenses or has used confusing syntax that a subtle alteration would improve, I will make corrections. But it is hard to establish rules; each case is slightly different. For example, Aimee's poem about the Civil War presented an interesting problem.

AFTER THE BATTLE

Bloody masses
of tangled legs
        and arms.
Copper casings
        glisten in the sun.
A blown out body
hangs half into a stream
        of crimson.
Which of you lost a leg?
        or two?
The slowly rising sun
is like the first shot,
Fired
and forgotten.

                        (*continued*)

FIGURE 4–3

Over the hill
       it comes,
as the flank came,
And over the grass
as it did yesterday
The grass no longer green,
the flank no longer a unit,
but a jumbled mass
of red
white
and blue.

    After someone in our class well versed in military history pointed out that copper casings had not been invented during the Civil War, Aimee's partner wanted to edit Aimee's line to correct the inaccuracy. I recommended that, before making the change, she get permission, but the dead-

FIGURE 4–4

Daddy Talks
by Susan Hodgin

Daddy talked of the great war
    at home
pulling that old silver trailer
with Mom and the three young boys
across those Southwest deserts
to Santa Anita for horses and work.

Daddy talked of the great war
    at home
struggling to make a living
as an exercise boy galloping
the horses around the oval track
getting ready for the opening day of the meeting.

Daddy talked of the great war
    at home
watching Momma sewing for the boys
cotton shirts from discarded flour sacks
and battling those moths that ate
holes in her trailer's cafe curtains.

Daddy talked of the great war
    across seas
helping government defense by painting
vehicle headlights half-black
to beam down to prevent aerial target
attacks from the western waters.

Daddy talked of the great war
    at home
canceling the meeting in 1942 and closing
the track to ship thoroughbreds out,
so Japanese-Americans could take
their manure smelling stalls in four days.

Daddy talked of the great war
    at home
shipping horses,
shipping trainers and groomsmen,
shipping Japanese-Americans like horses,
weaning them from their mother country.

Daddy talked of the great war
    at home
Listening hard to his life stories,
I was stunned by the confinement
of Americans, evicted from their homes
and robbed - like Daddy
was robbed - for just being here.

Dreams

Some people say that dreams are for fools. Me, I love to dream. I love to wander in those lands that only I can see. I can't really explain it. It's just a part of me.

Plush green trees and a summer breeze. Where the water is clean and beautifully clear. You may not see them, but the animals are there. Nobody in this land is hateful. They are full of love and happiness. Everyone is free to live as they please. The world is full of peace.

I know people think this is a silly and childish dream. But I believe in my heart that it just might come true. So I guess if dreams are for fools, then I am a fool, but personally, I believe that the real fool is the one that has never dreamed at all.

Brittany

As You Leave

My Sweet Little Baby
I watch you desperately
Seeking all the wonders I have sought
Finding all the treasures of life
Locked up
Within your own Sweet Heart.
Your beauty escapes you
And ignites my soul.
With joy and wonder
You reach for a new life
I can only dream of.

Sara

Old US 27:   Marshall, Michigan

She wakes from the sound of her own
breathing; exhales filling the empty room.
Familiar with loneliness-one
body sleeping where two
should be, she struggles
a yawn-heavy, wet air hanging
in her chest like forgotten laundry
trapped in a rainstorm.

Passing by her vanity she glimpses
her reflection, studying the map
of her happiness. Dressed in cool, white cotton
she eases dishonest summer blondness into
the teeth of a tortoiseshell comb.
Leaving the solitude
of their abondoned bedroom
she retreats to the garden
he plowed for her last fall.

Gathering her skirt between her
bronzed legs, she loosely knots it
and crouches barefoot straddling the soldierly rows of vegetables.
She dedides the beans need her and
actually enjoys bean picking;
relieving the leaves of their
weighty burden. Hands move
methodically right, pluck, drop
left, pluck, drop conducting
a symphony into the
bottomless bean bucket. Dry
red dust swirls around her
aware of the fine hairs sticking
to the nape of her neck,
sweat cradling her underarms, the
crooks of her knees.

The porchswing moans over her
snapping the beans-snapping and
rocking, measuring the afternoon's
passing by the swelling of
bite-sized bean bits in
the iron Dutch oven.

Beth

FIGURE 4–5

Spring Is Finally Here

Spring is finally here;
  I can hear the air   far and near.

The big blue sky is crystal clear
  So I can stare off into the atmosphere.

We can now cheer,
  But the snow will return next year. . . .

Nicholas

line was too near for the request to be made through an exchange of letters. So the partner telephoned Aimee's teacher, who gave her Aimee's phone number. Aimee agreed to change the line to "Brass colored buttons."

Another important lesson my students learn is that how text is presented can enhance or detract from the writing itself. Too many graphics, too flowery a font, too cramped a border can take the reader's eye away from the piece. However, using borders can enhance the uniqueness of separate works when they are on the same page or help a piece by itself standout.

The size, shape, and arrangement of the text can add drama. The flavor of Nicholas' rhyme, for example, is enhanced by graphics (Figure 4–5).

Not all art photocopies well, especially on certain machines. Reproduction that is too dark or grainy may be worse than no art. Photographs must be copied using halftone. Also, large areas of gray or black may copy unevenly, leaving faded or blotchy spots or streaks, making the text hard to read. In creating my own pages, I've found that filled-in borders can make the print seem blurred and the text hard to read. White text on black can be effective, but it is not always clear if the font is ornate. Generally, the simpler the font the better, although some creative chaos can add a playful quality to the anthology that young people enjoy (Figure 4–6).

Because there is so much to learn about what looks good and what does not, I encourage my students to examine past anthologies for ideas. I tell them to create draft pages first to see how everything will print and to check for readability. The governing question is, "do the layout, arrangement, illustrations, and fonts showcase the writers' work?" The writing should be featured, enhanced, complemented.

FIGURE 4-6

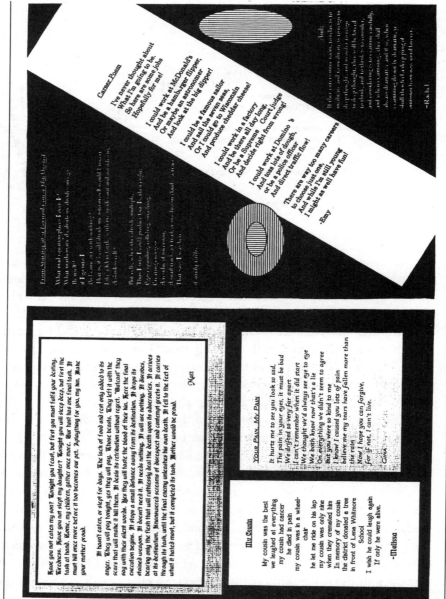

Career Poem

I've never thought about
What I'm going to be.
So here are some jobs
Hopefully for me!

I could work at McDonald's
And be a hamburger flipper,
Or maybe an astronomer
And look at the big dipper!

I could be a famous sailor
And sail the seven seas,
Or I could go to Wisconsin
And produce cheddar cheese!

I could work in a factory
And be there all day long,
Or be a Supreme Court judge
And decide right from wrong!

I could work at Domino's
And toss lots of dough,
or be a police officer
And direct traffic flow!

There are way too many careers
to choose just one,
And while I'm still young
I might as well have fun!

-Ray

From Meaning of a Legend (on a third friend)

What mad equation places I ever I?
What mathematical absolute in death can go
By itself?
of I emit I
Welcome art with authority
That is of small divide on internal I would I meet
I its 4 kind soul, with its medics out and outside em.
A body will I

But silly where the clock, multiple,
The I met I and I produce but I, thought I.
I geo-egmting collecting, exultating
Guating, coming
A really of increase,
A small trait, a gift on medicuos had extras
That is, I we lost

A milly trifle

And:

If the entire miss twins too far, too late is to
medicate, and to mediate its strength in
in depth, too, the cell, the head is so say
to think, and to think, is to essential,
and consulting, to tex, comm, carefully,
and when comm to, the shall
comming, down is dramatic, ye
shall the feel and epping of
imposs them now and forever.

-Rachel

Have you not eaten my son? Tonight you feast, but first you must fulfill your destiny. Tiredness, Have you not slept my daughter? Tonight you will sleep deep, but first the task at hand. Come, my children, gather once more. Our host has one final task. It must kill once more before it too becomes our pet. A plaything for you, my kin. Make your mother proud.

It hasn't eaten, or slept for days. The lack of food and rest only added to its anger. They will pay tonight, yes they will pay. Whose beasts. They left it with the scars that will make it kill them. It deals its retribution without regret. "Outcast" they say with their silent words. Yes they will taste the blood of their kin. Here the final execution begins. It stops a small distance away from its destination. It drops its stained weapon. It doesn't need it. It needs nothing. It will use nothing. It devolves, bearing only the flesh that will ruthlessly deal the death upon its adversaries. It arrives at its destination. Unmeasured screams of disrespect and contempt greets it. It carries through its task, until the final enemy unleashes his own death. It fell to the feet of what it hated most, but it completed its task. Mother would be proud.

Matt

My Cousin

My cousin was the best
we laughed at everything
my cousin had cancer
he died in pain
my cousin was in a wheel-
chair
he let me ride on his lap
my cousin was only nine
when they cremated him
In memory of my cousin
the district donated a tree
in front of Lena Whitmore
School
I wish he could laugh again
If only he were alive.

-Melissa

Your Pain, My Pain

It hurts me to see you look so sad,
The pain in your eyes, it must be bad
We drifted so very far apart
I can't remember when it did start
We thought we'd always see eye to eye
We both know now that's a lie
On everything we didn't seem to agree
But you were so kind to me
I know I caused you lots of pain
believe me my tears have fallen more than
the rain
Now I hope you can forgive,
for if not, I can't live.

-Gina

Perhaps the biggest lesson for my students is how hard it is to make writing error-free. Everyone knows how difficult it is to proofread his own material, and for that reason, I encourage my students to carefully scan each others' pages. Even then, I have not had one anthology yet perfect, partly because the production time is short and, at the end of the semester, college students are extremely busy. Those whose home computers do not have the desired fonts or graphics find the campus computers too far away or occupied. Careful proofreading takes two people and more time than some students have (or take). I have considered asking for submissions earlier to give ourselves more time, but writers do not have enough material from which to select earlier in the semester. So we simply put up with the occasional yet inevitable missing apostrophe, misspelled homonym, or lay/lie confusion and are grateful if these are the worst we get.

Once the pages are as perfect as each student can make them in the allotted time, they are turned over to a group of volunteer editors who organize the final anthology. These editors have several tasks. First, they decide on a theme and title. (The group that titled their anthology *Rustlings of Thought* selected leaves as a unifying theme and put pictures of trees on the front and back covers and tree graphics on each page. Another set of editors used graphics of planets and stars, and one group chose footprints.) Next, they arrange the pages in a roughly coherent order. Sometimes they try to mix poetry and prose, shorter and longer work, happy and somber themes, or they place works on similar topics together. Usually, the editors try to open and close the anthology with pieces that fit the theme, are about writing itself, or are particularly attention-getting, like Zac's "Poems" and Ralph Zeigler's "The Balladeers" (Figure 4-7).

Editors may insert additional illustrations and combine short works by cut-and-paste techniques to save space. Last, they type or paste on page numbers and create a table of contents. While they are doing these tasks, they check each piece for any obvious typos or other errors, and if they find ones they cannot easily correct, they call the person who created those pages and ask for them to be remade. (We have had some last-minute, late night phone calls, and even corrections done by correction fluid and typeover.) The editors also have the task of choosing the cover color and type of binding, and they have the privilege of being mentioned in the introduction.

Although producing the anthology is challenging and fun, problems are inevitable. One difficulty we always encounter is the failure of a few writers to submit writing by the deadline, whether because of absence or simple forgetfulness. Reminders are absolutely necessary. In addition to the written

FIGURE 4–7

The Balladeers	Poems
We are the ones who write for fun Even pen the path of a hearse Our pages are red with the maimed and the dead We will kill for the sake of the verse Our maidens sigh and cry and die As their pitiful tale is told There are heroes great who meet their fate And the bad men's souls are sold	I don't like poems I don't like poems I really really … Don't!! I don't read poems I don't read poems I really really… Don't!!
With our pens we whip the gun from the hip To give you the wild wild west Put a ship to sleep on the ocean deep And the Captain goes down with the rest Our tales of horror and splashes of gore Fill page after page after page Bodies are strewn from room to room By a mother who dies in a rage	I can't write poems I can't write poems I really really … Can't!!
There are wild wild tales of raging gales And youth returning fountains Earthquakes, snakes and poison lakes And hot erupting mountains But we can't entertain with all our pains The reader of today For even a song, if ten lines long Is sure to be cast away	I think they're dumb I think they're dumb I think they're really really … Dumb!!

announcements and requests for submission, a large sign posted in each classroom with the due date helps. Other effective reminders are an announcement placed in the school's bulletin and a large envelope clearly marked "For the Anthology" next to a check-off list of writers' names placed conspicuously near the classroom door. Once the deadline has passed, the teachers telephone students who still have not submitted their material, and on desperate occasions, such as a young writer's prolonged absence, a teacher will submit writing from the student's portfolio. I believe it is very important to include all writers in the anthology unless a writer expressly wishes to be left out. Only once has any of our writers declined to be included.

Another problem we sometimes face is writing that is potentially offensive or disturbing in a school-authorized publication. Fortunately, I have experienced this only twice. In both cases, I thought long and hard before making a decision. In one incident, a college student submitted, in camera-ready form, part of a short story that included a character's saying "Life's a bitch" and swearing "Christ!" Because of the conservative nature of some members of our community and so as not to offend *any* prospective reader of the anthology and endanger the project, I decided to cut the material. Because the story was incomplete (it was too long to be printed in its entirety), it could be ended at any point; so I simply excised the last line of the story that contained the curse. And, feeling like a guilty censor, I taped four typed dots over the other word, so the line read "Life's a . . . ." The writer had no objection, and no one had to retype the entire piece. In another episode, a junior high girl submitted a poem in which the persona describes suicide as "the only way out." Despite the inclusion of an author's note explaining that these were not her feelings but those of a friend who chose death over an unhappy life, her teacher and I agreed that the poem was best left out. Our school district is extremely cautious about any material that appears to make suicide attractive, and this particular poem could have been interpreted as treating suicide as a reasonable alternative. The teacher discussed our decision with the writer, who understood and gave us another poem to include.

Selling the Anthologies
Once we know exactly how many pages the anthology will be, we identify a per-book cost and take orders. In Figure 4-8 are two examples of handouts we give students, along with a teacher's order form.

We learned that collecting the money in advance works best, although some writers invariably forget their money on the day it is due. Sending around a list for writers to sign if they intend to buy an anthology helps us know how many to order, even if the money is late. And because some people who initially do not want an anthology change their minds once they see how it looks, I order from the copy service several more books than are spoken for. Extras also can be run after the initial production.

Obtaining Outside Funds
I sometimes receive small amounts of money to lower the per-book cost. My department contributes a little each semester, and when we produced a separate anthology for seventeen fifth- and sixth-grade writers, the principal paid the entire cost for each child's book. I have been reluctant to use advertising as a way to lower the price, primarily because I want the books to feature the writers and not be cluttered by ads. But ads are an attractive option if writers cannot afford to pay for their books. Also, selling advertising space, particularly to local merchants, is another way to involve the community with the schools and to garner support for community writing. I think many merchants would contribute willingly for a small space.

FIGURE 4-8

WRITING PARTNERS

THE ANTHOLOGY IS COMING

ONLY $2.50

PLACE YOUR ORDER WITH MRS. HODGIN TODAY

FILL OUT YOUR NAME BELOW AND GIVE THIS FORM TO MRS. HODGIN WITH $2.50 CASH OR A CHECK MADE OUT TO CAMPUS COPIES NO LATER THAN THE END OF SCHOOL MONDAY

IF YOU DO NOT ORDER ONE IN ADVANCE YOU MAY NOT GET ONE
LIMITED SUPPLY—RESERVE YOURS TODAY

YES, I WANT TO ORDER AN ANTHOLOGY

NAME _____
PERIOD _____

CHECK OR CASH PAID _____

Attention Writing Partners

Would you like to purchase the anthology of your and your Writing Partners' Writing?

If you would like to see yourself in print and purchase your very own copy of this entertaining volume guaranteed to *delight*, amuse, and astound, bring cash or a check made out to **U. of I. COPY CENTER*** in the amount of **$1.00 (per anthology)** to your English teacher **by Monday morning, December 12**. I will pick up all orders at NOON on Monday.

You will receive your anthology on **Wednesday, December 14**, at the reception. If you cannot attend the reception, please let me know, and I will arrange to deliver your anthology to your teacher.

*Parents: please be sure your local phone number is on the check.

Teacher _____

WRITING PARTNERS ANTHOLOGIES $1.00 ea.

Name	Number Ordered	Amt. Received

TOTAL # ANTHOLOGIES ORDERED _____   TOTAL ENCLOSED _____

Variations on the Anthology

I have always wanted to include the young writers in the production of the anthology and am still looking for a way to do this. If all (or even a large group) of the partners were in one class in one school, they could produce the anthology for a class project. But because our project is voluntary, and because the partners are in different classes usually with different teachers, the publication would have to be done in students' spare time, during lunch or after school, which is difficult for those active in clubs, organizations, and sports. If many of the partners are also members of a school writing club, the club might take on the production if it is not engaged in publishing a school literary magazine or newspaper. Another strategy the teachers and I are considering is to invite interested young writers to serve as co-editors alongside the college student editors. The group would meet outside school and share in the decisions about theme, title, and organization. In this way, the book would be a true collaboration.

A newsletter is an option to an anthology and might be more feasible if the writing partnerships last longer than a semester. In addition, a newsletter enables partners to read more of each others' writing during the year and gives writers something to look forward to regularly. It can encourage and inspire both younger and older writers, prod tardy writers to keep up, and attract other writers to the project. Ideally, a newsletter should be published about once a month, with each issue featuring writing by several sets of partners (along with brief biographies collected at the beginning of the semester with the other forms). Every writer in the project should be represented over the course of the year. As with the anthology, a team of editors can type and edit the writing, add illustrations, and so on.

Probably the most efficient method of producing a project newsletter is for the teacher and/or the project director and/or an editorial board to choose the partners' writing that will be featured in each issue. I would be reluctant to solicit submissions for a monthly newsletter for several reasons. First, given the problems I have experienced getting a few younger partners to submit material for the anthology on time, some students would miss the deadlines and never be published. Second, posting deadlines and collecting submissions is time-consuming. Third, some writers submit writing eagerly, but others are more reluctant. Thus, if submissions are voluntary, a newsletter might end up featuring the same writers over and over (I have seen school literary magazines that suffer from too much by too few) and not showcase everyone. Fourth, a newsletter might discourage young partners from sharing writing with their partners for fear that it might be published.

Some writers only want their partner and teacher to read their work and could feel uncomfortable writing for a more public audience. One of the values of the project is that it allows writers to share work in progress, to take risks, to send writing about which the author is uncertain. A newsletter, even one designed specifically to feature incomplete work, might subvert these aims.

The Reception

Imagine a school library crowded with fifty or sixty people whose ages range from fourteen to eighty-two, sitting at round tables, nibbling cookies and drinking pop, turning pages of an anthology, and talking. Everyone in the room is a writer; everyone here loves to write and is proud of it. The writers have come not only out of curiosity to meet the people to whom they have been sharing writing for the past several months, but also to celebrate, to acknowledge the pleasure writing brings to their lives. These receptions, held at the end of each semester, allow partners to get acquainted face to face and to read and hear, also for the first time, the work of other writers in the project.

Planning for the reception begins early in the semester and, in a way, establishes the calendar for the end of each project. The teachers and I examine the school calendar, select a date that will not be in conflict with other school or community events, and reserve a room for approximately two hours, depending on the number of writing partners. The library at our junior high is an ideal location, for it is spacious enough to hold fifty-plus people, yet small enough to encourage close seating and the sense of an intimate community. (When elementary school writers are in the project, we hold separate receptions at the school either during the day or at night, with parents invited.) Once the date and room for the reception are determined, I set the date the anthology must go to the printer, since the distribution of the anthologies takes place at the reception. Then, by backing up ten days to give the editorial group time to collate and design the book and to allow teachers to collect orders, I determine the date when my students must have their camera-ready pages for the editors. By again backing up a week or ten days, I have the deadline for submissions. Thus, all these dates can be determined early in the project once the reception date is known.

As the date for our party approaches, partners look forward to meeting each other. To avoid the disappointment of one partner's absence, the teachers and I go to great lengths to ensure everyone's presence. Very early in the semester, once I know the date, I notify community writers in a memo:

To: All Community/College Writing Partners
From: Candida Gillis
Date: 9/28/96
RE: End of Semester Reception

Plan ahead! On December 13, from 7 to 9 PM, we will host a reception
for you and your partners at the Moscow Junior High School Library.
This is the occasion where you will meet your partner, receive an anthology if you have ordered one, and listen to your fellow partners read
excerpts of their writing. Your partner will be counting on your coming.
Please make arrangements to attend for at least some of the time. The
evening will be well worth your while. Thanks!

    Three weeks before the reception, I send each partner a "formal" invita-
tion, illustrated in Figure 4-9. Then one week before the event, I send

FIGURE 4–9

You are invited to

A Reception

For all participants in the
Writing Partners Project

When: *Tuesday, May 7, 7-8:30 p.m.*

Where: *Moscow Junior High Library*

Come and meet your writing partner, enjoy
refreshments, and share your writing

Hosted by the U. of I. Writing Workshop class

another reminder to community writers included in a letter requesting an evaluation of the project:

> Dear Community Writing Partners,
>
> This semester's project will be ending soon. Your writing partners and I are grateful for your participation. Your willingness to share your writing with your partners and to encourage their work is invaluable in helping them see themselves as "real writers," like you.
>
> I am very interested in any comments you wish to share about your participation in the project. I would like to hear any thoughts you might have about what you, as a writer, gained from having a writing partner, or about how I might improve the project in the future.
>
> Would you be interested in having another partner in the fall?
>
> *Thank you again, and I will see you at the reception next week. (The Junior High reception is at 7:00 in the Junior High Library, May 10; the elementary reception is at 3:15 in the Russell School Library on May 9.) If for some reason you will be unable to attend the reception, please let me know so I can tell your partner.*

College partners write personal notes to their partners telling them they are looking forward to meeting them at the reception, and teachers talk to each of their students stressing the importance of coming. (Susan tells her students that they are excused from the reception only if they are dead or giving birth.) If a writer cannot attend (one partner had to attend her own bridal shower), we ask the community writer to call the partner's teacher and make arrangements to meet the partner at his or her school. With all these reminders, we have near perfect attendance!

The reception itself is simple to run. The program of getting acquainted, snacking, looking at the anthology, and reading takes about one-and-one-half to two hours, not including cleanup. My students and I bring the food and drink, the less messy the better to spare the library floor (popcorn and potato chips are out). We put all the food and beverages on one table and arrange the other tables and chairs so they are spaced closely enough to encourage talk, yet open enough to allow people to move back and forth from the food table to their seats. A music stand serves as a podium and is placed strategically so everyone can see and hear the readers. As people arrive, the teachers and I call out names so writers can locate their partners, and we distribute anthologies to those who have paid. Although parents are not specifically invited, some come, just as interested in meeting the partners as their sons or daughters.

I always enjoy watching partners meet for the first time. Some are shy at first, the young ones reluctant to leave their age-mates until encouraged. A few bring presents for their partners—a picture of themselves, a "thank you" card, a flower, new writing they want their partner to read. As people begin to talk and grow more comfortable, the teachers and I, in an effort to establish a comfortable, informal mood, encourage everyone to get food at any time and to sit with their partners if they are not doing so already. The anthology is an excellent icebreaker, as partners eagerly look up the pages with their writing and that of friends, excited to see how it appears. This is a moment of truth for the editors and the partners who prepared the polished pages, because the layouts and proofreading are carefully scrutinized. My students listen for every comment, alert for criticism or compliment, dreading "Hey, you spelled my name wrong!" or "Whoa, did anyone spell-check this?"

Once everyone has arrived (a few partners invariably come late for one reason or another) and is settled, I make a few comments about the project, thanking everyone for coming and the teachers for their help. Then we applaud the editors for their work on the anthology (each semester's always seems to be the best yet), and I introduce the more formal aspect of the program, the readings. We have two ground rules for the readings: 1) everyone must come to the "podium" and read a piece of his own writing (or of his partner's, if he feels too shy), either from the anthology or brought for the purpose; 2) no one should take longer than three minutes (longer pieces should be excerpted). From this point on, the evening belongs to the writers. Readers are usually reluctant at first and need some encouragement from their teachers or from me, but once two or three people have read, others are anxious to follow, and we rarely have to urge. (Older writers are sometimes more hesitant than the younger writers.) Some writers want to read more than once, and one young writer was so enthusiastic he asked his teacher if he could go back to his classroom for his portfolio!

In the tradition of a celebration, we clap after each reading. The applause is genuine, for most readers read their writing with conviction and intensity; even works that seem flat or trite on the page can be transformed when the writers' voices interpret them. The poetry, fiction, and memoirs in the anthology become dramas. Writers sometimes cry when reading a particularly emotional and personal piece, and listeners, too, are moved. A writer may spontaneously add to a piece, revising on the spot. One writer's three short paragraphs about how he came to love hockey grew into a lively, detailed story when, as he was reading, he turned the line "I ended up getting hit in the thigh" into a lengthy, slightly off-color, and very funny monologue.

Lucy Calkins writes, "I write to hold what I find in my life in my hands and to declare it a treasure" (7). As an audience of writers, especially writers whose task it has been to support and encourage, we respond to each work we hear fully and appreciatively, knowing that it represents a treasure to be treated with respect and admiration, no matter how small. Sharing these treasures through the anthology and at the reception, and responding so positively to others', validates writers' commitments to their crafts. Everyone present feels a sense of belonging to a special community bounded not by age or occupation or social stratification or ethnicity, but by a common love of the arts of language. I leave every reception enriched by what I have heard and read, and inspired to write. So, I gather, do the writing partners and teachers.

Conclusions and Beginnings

The end of the semester is technically the end of the project. At the fall reception, some partners agree to continue their partnership into the spring semester; and some decide to write each other during the summer. Partners who continue into another school semester sign new contracts, but those who want to exchange writing over the summer do so on their own, outside the project's and the school's responsibility. To those partners (and the parents of the young partners) I send letters clarifying that the teachers and I are no longer responsible for overseeing the exchange of writing. Although this note sounds cold, it effectively absolves us of any responsibility for extracurricular partnerships:

> Dear Parent or Guardian of _____[young writer]:
>
> The Writing Partners Project officially ends [date]. Any future exchanges of writing between your son or daughter and her or his partner are the responsibility of you, your child, and his or her partner. The teachers and I are not responsible for picking up and delivering writing or overseeing the exchange in any way.

The end of the semester is also the time for thank yous, a time to solicit writers for the next project, and to collect evaluations (the forms are shown in Chapter 5). I am grateful to the writers in the community who take their time to share their work and their love of writing with a young writer, and I let them know through a personal "thank you." Here is a sample letter:

> Dear _____ [community writer],
>
> Thank you again for participating in the Writing Partners Project this semester. I, _____ [partner], and _____ [partner]'s teacher value greatly the time and energy you have given to helping _____ [partner] grow as a writer. By sharing your work and re-

sponding to his, you have let him know not only that his writing is valuable, but also that writing itself is a precious, lifelong, and worthy endeavor. We are all grateful for your comments and encouragement.

In the fall, we will have more young writers who would like partners. Would you like to participate in the project again with a new partner? Please let me know. Also, if you know another writer in the community who might be interested in participating, let me know his or her name and address. I will be happy to send him or her information about the project.

Appreciatively,
Candida Gillis
[Address, Phone #]

With letters like this one I have expanded the network of writers as well as expressed my appreciation for community writers' participation. Many writers choose to continue with new partners. Others drop out for one reason or another. One writer was disappointed that her partner was not more serious about her writing; another was unhappy with the amount of feedback her fifth-grade partner gave. I take responsibility for these writers' discontinuing; from them I learned the need to be very clear, when I describe the project to prospective writers, about young peoples' writing, their varying commitments and abilities to write and respond with depth and specificity, and the pressures on their time. Writers also discontinue not because they are dissatisfied with the project but because they move out of the area, become involved in other activities, or simply want to take a break. But as some drop out, new writers join.

Like the community writers, many young writers want to participate for more than one semester. Over half of the writers in the fall projects usually sign on again for the spring. Some dedicated partners stay with the project (with new partners) longer. One girl now in the tenth grade has had writing partners since the fifth grade, the year of the project's inception. Three others began the project in the eighth grade and stayed through the tenth. Having a writing partner is contagious; as word spreads, more and more young writers want to be involved. The teachers and I do not encourage writers to continue (although we do not discourage them) beyond one year so that we may give new students a chance to have partners; the demand for adult partners is generally greater than the supply. In a larger community, teachers might accommodate more students, although the larger the number of writers involved, the larger the task of administrating the project (particularly making initial contacts with writers and picking up and delivering writing), and the greater the need for clerical help. One year an assistant helped

FIGURE 4–10

address envelopes, drove around town, made signs for classes, and photocopied signs and other materials. This was the year I had the most and most widely dispersed partners—in several college classes, throughout the community, in three schools, and in eight teachers' classrooms. My assistant was invaluable. A teacher running a program of partnerships for her own students might enlist help from the school's clerical or secretarial staff and from the students themselves.

The end of the semester is the time to prepare for the next. Writers in the community should be contacted, updated letters of information for prospective partners prepared, the calendar for the reception and anthology established. This is also a time to review the evaluations and reflect on how the project worked, on what students and their partners gained, on what changes might be made to improve. Every semester I make slight modifications. The materials in this book are the result of five years of changes—improvements in the delivery system, in how I inform partners, in the production of the anthology, and more. Despite my successes in reaching my original goals, I constantly adjust, alter, fine-tune the project as I learn more and as the interests and needs of writers change.

5

The Partnership Experience: Reflections

"What did you learn from having a writing partner?"
"To write faster."

Having a writing partner is a unique experience for each pair of writers and for each partner. What a person gains from the experience varies, of course, in nature and intensity, and depends on factors such as personality of the writer, depth of commitment to writing, and amount of free time. For some, the partnership is deeply enriching, for others less fruitful; few gain nothing. At the very least, partners enjoy the adventure. Every semester I ask all partners, teachers, and the young writers' parents to tell me in writing (anonymously, if they wish) what they feel they, their children, or their students gain from having writing partners. The comments are overwhelmingly positive and include insights about audience, writing styles and techniques, self, and the world.

Rewards for Young Writers

What do novice writers gain from having a writing partner? Parents, teachers, and the young writers themselves have similar ideas. And what they reveal in their surveys is echoed in the actual writing and letters young writers send. Writing partnerships offer many different rewards not inconsistent with my initial goals for the project, as a sample of participants' and their parents' comments over the last several years illustrates.

Students' Views
Writers can learn as much about audiences as about their own writing. They discover that readers may not see their writing as they do:

> I think I gained a better understanding of my own writing and what other people think about it.

> Sometimes people don't react the way that you expect to your writing, and sometimes their perception is just as you had hoped, or even more so.

FIGURE 5–1a

WRITING PARTNERS: PROJECT EVALUATION
Fall, 1994

Dear Writing Partners:

Now that the semester is nearing the end, so is this semester's writing partners project. In order to make the project better next semester, I would like to hear from you. I would appreciate your taking a few minutes to answer the questions below. If you need more room to write, use the back of this page. <u>You do not have to write your name on this evaluation, but may if you wish</u>. PLEASE RETURN THIS FORM TO YOUR TEACHER BY DECEMBER 16. Thank you!

1.　How did you like participating in the project?

2.　What did you feel you learned from having a writing partner?

3.　What would you like to change about the project?

4.　Would you like to participate in the project again if you had the chance?

FIGURE 5–1b

WRITING PARTNERS: PROJECT EVALUATION
Fall, 1994

Dear Parents/Guardians of Writing Partners:

Now that the semester is nearing the end, this semester's writing partners project is winding down. In the spring I will be continuing the project, and in order to make it even better, I welcome your input. I would appreciate your taking a few minutes to answer the questions below. Please return the form to your son/daughter's teacher before December 20. Thank you!

1. Do you think your son/daugher enjoyed participating in the project?

2. Do you feel he or she benefited from having a writing partner? In what ways?

3. Is there anything you would like to see different about the project?

4. Would you like your child to participate in the project or a similar project again if he or she had the opportunity?

5. Any other suggestions, comments?

Many thanks.

Candy Gillis

I learned that I might miss things in my writing that might make sense to me, but might not to others.

Some grow to a deeper understanding of reading processes, of the transactions between reader and writer.

[I discovered that] my writing can evoke feelings of the reader and [that readers] can relate their own experiences.

I learned that people will interpret writings way off what you wrote the piece about. That's not necessarily a bad thing, just something to be careful about if it's especially important that you need to get your point across clearly. I've always thought that you shouldn't tell people what your writing's about (unless they're totally confused) because as they read it they bring a part of their life to it, relate to it. If they know what it's about, it might bring some of that out.

I've learned what people enjoy reading.

Having a writing partner can expand a young writer's awareness of styles, strategies, forms of writing, and subjects to write about. In addition, it can help a writer appreciate well-intentioned criticism.

I have gained a sense of respect for all forms of writing. And that many people have various ways of getting a point across.

I learned new ways to write poetry.

[I learned] I can write other styles of writing.

[Writing Partners] allowed me to expand the variety of my writing.

I was opened up to new ideas and different writing.

I learned how to turn my writing from a normal piece into something more creative. I learned to use more detail.

To stretch the language.

[I gained] new ideas and a friend. I got constructive criticism and comments on how to improve my writing.

That it's nice, and helpful, to get feedback from another person.

And partnerships can teach writers how to be better critics themselves:

I learned how to critique better and I got a new perspective on my writing.

I think I learned how to be honest in criticizing others' work. I also learned a lot of patience in waiting for my letters to arrive.

Confidence in one's self as a writer and in sharing writing is among the most-reported benefits of the project:

> I got a lot of praise on the things I wrote and now I'm more secure about myself and my writing.

> I felt I learned that my writing matters to other people, and that I have more creativity than I thought.

> I've gained more confidence in my writing. Just because one person (a friend) doesn't like it, doesn't mean my partner won't.

> [I learned] better letter writing and trust in someone you don't know. It's hard for me to give my writing to others—even people I know, but with my writing partner, it was different. I came to trust him and we became good friends.

> I'm not afraid to show people what I wrote.

Many people simply appreciate the opportunity to write and gain a better understanding of people and the world:

> [I liked] having a good excuse to write all the stories that I never got around to.

> My writing partner taught me things about proofreading, and what it would be like to be an English teacher.

> My writing partner showed me some of her work from when she was about my age and her work now, and how different they were.

> I learned that even college students majoring in English can make mistakes and it gave me a good reason to write again.

> Writing is fun.

Parents' Views

Parents are similar to the young writers in their descriptions of the project's benefits. They perceive that writing to an older partner gives their children more practice with writing, improved confidence and skills, and exposure to new types of writing. Parents seem to recognize the importance of having supportive, encouraging readers and of writing to real audiences beyond the classroom.

> Definitely she [benefited]; improved her English skills because we speak another language at home.

> I think her writing skills improved and she tried different types of material.

[The project] made her more focused in her writing.

It made her see more in poetry.

She enjoyed reading other people's writing, seeing a different style and gleaning ideas from someone other than a teacher.

The more one writes the more they gain. I think sharing with someone other than the teacher, the child might explore some ideas and styles knowing that there was not a grade attached.

Katherine liked having someone to share her writing with. The fact that it was an adult seemed to add an element of respect.

[The project] encouraged her to write more, gaining experience and confidence.

My child benefited by having someone who cares read and encourage her writing.

[The project] built confidence. She loves writing and sharing.

[Having a writing partner] was an excellent way of giving [my child] feedback on her writing from someone she isn't emotionally involved with.

She was able to learn about and become acquainted with someone she's never met. She could experience an older person's writing style(s).

[My son] received reinforcement for writing—saw it as a positive experience. He had a kind respondent who was sensitive to his feelings, gave him the feeling that he was understood and appreciated.

It built her confidence in her writing skills. Partly because even her older partner was unsure of the quality of her work, letting [my daughter] know that everyone asks "Is it any good?" and that we are always our own worst critic.

Very few partners or their parents write negative comments on the written evaluation. Liza, who wanted to write to her college partner privately (see Chapter 2), said she never understood Joe's writing anyway, and preferred writing to pen pals. Another student wrote that she wasn't clear what was expected of her. The single, most frequent complaint is that sometimes one must wait too long to hear from the partner. Dissatisfaction with partnerships is rarely expressed, possibly because anyone who is unhappy with the project usually drops out or changes partners early in a semester. The suggestions young writers make most often are for a quicker turnaround and the chance to meet their partners at the beginning of the semester. (In response to the first suggestion, I tried shortening the turnaround to one week with mixed results; some writers need more time. And I resist the idea of an earlier meeting simply because I believe there is more to be gained from being forced to respond solely to the writing and not to the face behind it. One must learn the personality of the partner and convey one's own self entirely through the writing.)

Indirect Benefits

Having a writing partner benefits young writers in ways that the writers themselves may not be conscious of but that are apparent in the letters and writing to their partners. One obvious benefit of the exchanges is the opportunity to reflect on and describe oneself as a writer. The result is that partners become more aware of composing strategies and the rhetorical aspects of writing itself—purpose and audience. The interchange between Saundra, a college senior, and her tenth-grade partner, Katie, whose introductory letters are included in Chapter 3, illustrates the kind of discussions about writing processes that partners often engage in. In her letter that follows, Saundra is responding to two of Katie's poems sent earlier in the exchange, "So What" and "Glowing Figures":

> So What
>
> I want to go somewhere,
>   where I can think
> Alone—Frightful beings
>   always surrounding me
>   with their own thoughts.
> I want to be able to know
>   what I am.
> No hassles,
>   forever—
> Can't that happen?
> According to McDonald's, it can.
> So what.

> Glowing Figures
>
> Lighting, glowing figures—wanting nothing in a
>   world of nothing—cameras—flashing bulbs—
>   world of lights spinning around—
>   running into each other.
> Twist, turn, fall down,
>   then rise above to conquer.
> Glowing figures can do that.

Dear Katie,

Thanks so much for your letter and poems. I often prefer to write poetry in my own handwriting as well. Even though I know they are much easier to read when typed, they just seem so stiff and formal.

Your poems both really interested me. The first one, "So What," kind of reminded me of something I would write. The lines "I want to be able to know/what I am" seemed especially similar to my poetry. I like to write down my thoughts in this type of abstract manner. (I hope I am making some sense!!) "Glowing Figures" was really vivid for me. I like how you wrote it kind of abruptly: "world of nothing—cameras—flashing bulbs." It gave the poem a tense feeling, not only because of your actual words but because of the structure you used as well.

The poem I'm sending you this time, "Questions," reminds me a bit of "So What." I kind of set up an idea (the idea of someone questioning me or prying into my life), and then, like, you, I finish the poem with almost an abrupt slam. It seems as if both of us were closing a door to our thoughts. How do you feel about that analysis? (I know . . . pretty strange, huh?)

Well, I can't wait to hear what your thoughts are. Thanks again for sharing your poetry with me!

Sincerely,
Saundra

QUESTIONS

Inquiring minds want to know,
Everything they can;
Everything they shouldn't.
They beg . . . they plead,
And you answer back,
        because you know not what to do.
It takes a lot to
        deny the windbreak of information
Floating between you and society.
I can't stand the urge I have
        to overcome your greedy finger,
        poking into my business.
Some day I'll let it go—
Out where you can catch it.
        Not today.

Katie responds:

Dear Saundra,

I totally understand what you said about my poems. I do like to write abstractly. Most of my poems are just strange thoughts written down quite quickly. I really identify with your poem "Questions." I feel this way a lot. The way you described the ending of yours and my poems with "an abrupt slam" really makes sense to me. Most of the poems I write end this way. Some though fade away.

The poem I sent you this time, "Thoughts," ends kind of in this way. I wanted it to fade away. I hope you like it and please tell me what you think of it.

Sincerely,
Katie

THOUGHTS

Solitary thoughts.
Feelings underneath, behind,
Hiding, closing the door.

Comparative thoughts.
Lightness flowing,
Never knowing, gone.

Flying thoughts.
Lying, not true, falling.
Closer, and more closer.

Saundra's response to Katie's poem is explicit and personal:

"Thoughts" seemed to have a sad tone to it. When I read your second and third lines ("Feelings underneath, behind,/ Hiding, closing the door"), I felt almost a sensation of being trapped. Last night my boyfriend came to visit and he and I were having a sort-of heated "discussion." He started getting mad at me because he said I was closing my thoughts up. This reminded me exactly of your poem. I seemed to be hiding my thoughts and pulling him away from them even though I really wanted to open up to him. Does this make any sense? It was just amazing how the words in your poem seemed to describe me perfectly last night.

The depth with which Saundra responds shows Katie how her writing comes to have meaning for a reader. Saundra also provides context for her own work by explaining how she came to write "Questions" and how the poem related to Katie's. In response, Katie attempts to examine how she writes. As she explains in a later letter, "When I write most of my poems they are just random thoughts. All of those that I have sent you are just like that. I usually don't know how to interpret them but the way you describe and interpret them really makes sense to me."

Like Katie, other young writers take the cue from their partners and explain how their writing was conceived:

I'm also sending what I think to be one of my strongest short stories, "Of Darkness and Comets." My family is part of a church-related group that gets together each month to eat. Each January we go to Moscow Mt. to sled. It's terrific fun, and this is the story of what happened one day.

This story I'm sending was started on the last day of basketball tryout. I was scared, nervous, and sick all day. I felt like I was going to die. I'm sorry the manuscript is so sloppy. I barely got your letter and haven't had time to revise it more than once. Please be very careful with it, it's my only copy. I hope you can read my writing.

For my writing, I'm sending you the essay I sent in for the impromptu DWA (Direct Writing Assessment). The prompt was to write about a concern you have for the future. If you take the essay literally, it is a humorous essay, but if you read carefully, maybe you'll see the underlying meaning. Please tell me your thoughts while reading it.

Like Saundra and Katie, Lindy and Angela exchange ideas about writing, explain their own writing processes, and convey how the other's work affects them. They are receptive also, interested in learning about writing, literature, and each other. Lindy is an older college student returning to school after many years of work and childrearing; her partner, Angela, is an eighth grader (her introductory letter to a later partner, Russ, is included in Chapter 3). In her opening "Dear Writing Partner" letter, Lindy writes seriously about writing, a tone Angela adopts:

Dear Writing Partner,

This is to say hello and tell you a little about myself. I am a "non-traditional" returning student, back in school after many years in the work world. My major is English with a literature emphasis and my minor is Spanish. Writing is a special interest and love. It will be fun to read your writing and I'm looking forward to it. It's always valuable to see how another writer expresses ideas and what they find "observable" in life.

If you have any questions or want me to pay attention to any special aspect of your writing, please feel free to ask. I'll be asking you for your input about my work too. Do you have a favorite author? What is your favorite thing to write about? Have you ever kept a journal?

I'm looking forward to hearing from you and receiving your writing sample. This semester will be more fun because I now have a writing partner!

Bye for Now,
Lindy

In successive letters Lindy describes some prewriting strategies she uses. Angela is receptive and shares her own self-analysis:

Lindy,

Thank you so much for the story title ideas! I'm not quite sure about a name just yet, but your thoughts definitely helped me get some new ideas rolling.

For my next story, I'm going to start out by trying that outlining idea of yours.

I did something a lot like that in 7th grade for English class, but the story didn't turn out as well as I had hoped it would. (Unfortunately, the outline ended up being better and more elaborate than the story—who knows why.) But I'll give it another shot (maybe this time it'll work out).

I already jot down key words and phrases to help me along—but that's just so I don't forget something important when it comes time to start actually writing. Hopefully, outlining will save me both time and grief.

I remember one night when I was lying in bed and a new story idea just popped into my head, basically out of nowhere. I didn't want to forget anything, and I didn't have any regular paper on hand, so I grabbed a pencil off of my dresser and started writing away on the only thing I could find—the calendar above my bed. (The next morning, my story was there, but March wasn't.)

The poem that I'm working on right now started out as an outline also. See, for some reason, I usually find that I have a harder time just writing free-form poetry than I do with writing stories off the top of my head (don't ask me why), so I pretty much just take basic outlines and change them around a little to add my own style as I go along. (You'll get to see what I mean with my latest piece in the works, "She Is.")

As you can probably tell, poetry is pretty new to me (I learned to enjoy it last year while reading pieces by Langston Hughes and Maya Angelou in class and at home).

Well, I'd better go work on my poem some more. (The copy you are receiving is an incomplete first draft), so if you have any suggestions or questions, feel free to let me know.

Angela

P. S. I can't seem to be able to come up with any specific situations or ideas for your new story, but one thing I was thinking about was maybe having the girl grow up, constantly in the shadow of someone else, but finally overcoming that and becoming someone great.

P. P. S. I love "Let Me Help You"! The surprise ending was great!

Angela is articulate about her writing and self-aware. Her interest in reading as well as writing prompts Lindy to continue a discussion of authors and make some recommendations:

FIGURE 5–2a

SHE IS

She is an optomistic teenager living
   in a battlezone
She wonders why the shooting never stops
She hears the thunder of the .38, the
   shattering clang of the breaking glass,
   the victim's screams, and the screeching
   of the tires as the assailants get away, once again
She sees the all too familiar yellow tape
   fencing the sidewalk what seems like everyday
She wants to be away from it all - free from
   the hurt and the pain
She is an optomistic teenager living in a
   battlezone

She prays that the awe of "Ghetto Star" and "O.G."
   status will never draw her or her
   brothers and sisters in
She feels the cold & eerie emptyness come
   over her as yet another close friend is buried
She touches ???
She worries about whether or not the war will
   someday hit her
She cries herself to sleep at night - hoping
   that tomorrow will be better
She is an optomistic teenager living in a battle
   zone

She understands that it can all change - even though it seems as if it may never change
She says that things shouldn't be that
   way - that "soon it'll be different"
                                    →

FIGURE 5–2b

She dreams of a world without gangbangers,
    drug dealers, or junkies
She tries to stay strong
She hopes she'll always be strong
She is an optomistic teenager living in a
    battlezone

She wonders what she did wrong – what
    she could have done to stop it
Yet she knows the answer... "nothing"
She hates those ignorant people who hide
    behind false words and phrases like
    "truce" and "it's their own fault"
Yet she knows that they just don't
    understand – they refuse to understand
She pretends that it doesn't exist – that
    everything's perfectly alright
Yet she knows that it's far from alright
    or normal. It's all just gotten too
    real – out of control like a giant
    snowball rolling down a hill

You may ask : "who is she" and "what does
    she have to do with me?"
The truth?
She is the leftovers – an outcast of society –
    an innocent victim
Say what?
Yeah, you heard me. She shouldn't have to
    escape to the suburbs to experience
    peace. It shouldn't make a difference
    whether she lives in Compton or Bel Air →

but it does, and she has everything to
do with you...

    She is our Future

Dear Angela,

Your poem expresses the mood of despair and hopelessness that "She" has to contend with just trying to make it through the day. I'm interested to see the polished piece when you finish it. Maya Angelou was an early influence on my love of poetry too! Have you read any of her autobiographies? Another wonderful Afro-American poet is Ruth Forman, and I looked up one of hers to send to you. [A Copy of "Poetry Should Ride the Bus" follows (*We Are the Young Magicians*. Boston: Beacon Press, 1993, pp. 10-11).]

Lindy

P. S. Still working on the never-ending story. Now have to figure out a way to get [the characters] back into the present and finish!

It is not uncommon for writing partners' dialogues to include discussion of books and authors; writers are readers, too, and enjoy sharing favorites and making recommendations. When this happens, the writers become "reading partners," as Angela and Lindy do.

Dear Lindy,

Thank you for sending me that poem by Ruth Forman. I had never heard of her before your letter, but I really loved that piece "Poetry Should Ride the Bus," and I'm going to try to find some more of her work at the library.

I haven't read any of Maya Angelou's autobiographies yet, but my mom has a couple of her books here at home—I guess I just haven't gotten around to seriously reading any of them. I was just thinking about how much my attitude towards writing has changed over the years. I mean, not even two years ago, I couldn't even hear the word "poetry" without making some kind of gagging sound or gesture. But now, I really like the stuff!

Have you ever gone through this type of thing, where one minute, you can't stand something, and then suddenly, you love it, but you aren't really sure how you grew to love it?

Now, I'm not even sure why I used to hate poetry so much. I mean, sure—there are those poems that are just plain dumb, boring, and simply not worth diddley squat, but then again, that's also true of books. Who knows—this may just be a phase, but I plan on enjoying it while I can.

Just recently, I started reading the lost poetry and writings of the late musician Jim Morrison. I really like his pieces because they seem REAL. You know what I mean? Not just fancy words or rhyming phrases, but reality. His writing and songs are about life, and everyone interprets life differently—that's what makes it unique and special; and I think that that's how poetry should be. Without rules or guidelines. Everyone should read something different into it.

Our school's art teacher feels that same way (it's one of his books that I'm borrowing). For one of his assignments, he picked two of Morrison's poems, read them to all of his Art I students, and had them sketch out what they felt. Now he has the best drawings hanging up in the halls, and what's cool about that is that every picture is different, and conveys a different feeling.

Different is good.

Angela

Lindy and Angela's partnership continues to explore favorite authors and in the process, they share more about themselves. Angela's fondness for Jim Morrison evokes a strong response:

Hi Angela,

I'm glad that you liked Forman's stuff. I got into such a habit of reading her that when I loaned the book to my friend I really missed it! She's very young and new to the publishing scene, so don't know if she'd be in the library, but good ole Book People does have her on the shelf. Probably your new love of poetry has come because you are at an age where you can choose who and what kind to look for. When I was forced in school to read a certain type of poetic writing before I was ready, I hated it! For me, trying to write in a certain genre also helps to understand the force behind it. Poetry is so distilled and immediate and such a great way to try to understand feelings (both my own and other people's).

I was around when Jim Morrison first started performing and liked his literate approach to chaos. He was a talented writer and it's a shame that he indulged himself to death and we are deprived of his talent. The immediacy of his poetry is pretty intense and I can understand why it would be a great art project to try to translate him in this medium. I agree with you that different is good and I believe difference is what makes our country such a fascinating and multi-layered place. Sometimes people don't want to understand the complexity involved with other cultures, but it's worth the time and effort to try to understand each other. So much for the soap box. I'm late as usual—so—I remain— Your Writing Partner.

Lindy

Angela does revise "She Is"; the final version is at the end of this chapter. Many partners, like Lindy and Angela, share likes, dislikes, passions, and thoughts and discover much they have in common besides their love of writing. And that is another reward of having a partner who is of a different age—the wonderful surprise of making connections, of finding shared understandings, experiences, values. Chance, a college student, and Anneli, whose letter to her later partner, Hilary, ends Chapter 3, discover a major interest in sports and a mutual appreciation of each others' writing; they build each other's confidence.

Dear Chance,

Hello. I'm sorry I haven't written you sooner, but I've been busy with sports and school work. And this fine Sunday afternoon is the only time I've had time. Well anyway, my name is Anneli and I'm in the 8th grade. I really enjoyed your essay because I too love football. And, even though I'm a girl, I've always played and loved all sports. Aside from sports I enjoy being a normal fun-loving 13 year old and spending time with my many friends (who are mainly boys) and since I've lived in Moscow all my life there's not much else to do. I'm sending you a poem I wrote and with it the format in which I wrote it. Try to keep in mind that I wrote it to be somewhat funny and playful. Well anyway I'll make sure to write you again by Friday and tell you all I thought about your essay, but for now it's on to homework.

Yours truly,
Anneli

Chance responds:

Dear Anneli,

I liked your poem! Sometimes poems that don't rhyme have to have a meaning, or something, to make them sound good. Yours has that, and I could see a lot of places where it really flows great! I liked the part in the first verse, "I see his smile and eyes lit bright, and I need to hold him close at night." Those "i" sounds really bring kind of a "song" effect to it, how well it flows. Was this created from a true inspiration by someone, or did you make it for anyone in general?

I have a note attached to your poem [from me] saying that you're on the eighth grade football team. Awesome! Football is one of the greatest games of our time and it shouldn't be limited to one gender. Everyone should experience it. What position(s) do you play? In Riggins we were only offered four years of football, so there was no junior high football. My freshman year I played tight end on offense and linebacker on defense. That's how it went until my senior year, when I started games as: running back, tight end, wide receiver, but mostly guard. On defense I was a defensive end. We play eight-man football, which is both easier and harder than eleven-man.

This little piece that I'm writing is describing my first rapid of my first whitewater training trip. Two friends of mine, Steve and Matt, were my high-siders. High-siders are people (usually guests) who shift their weight in the boat opposite the direction of the waves that are hitting it. The first set of rapids are called Ruby Rapids, which get quite famous in the high-waters of spring.

FIGURE 5–3

I AM

I am sad and lonely.
At times I wonder what love is, And why
I love, or think I love him.
I can hear his voice through my head.
I See his Smile and eyes lit bright, and
I need to hold him close at hight, for
I am sad and lonely.

I can only pretend to be close to
him, and at times I feel his breath.
I reach out and hold his hands, worrying
he doesn't feel the Same way.
I cry when I think of not knowing
him, cause.
I am Sad and lonely.

I understand that I'm just a child,
but I Say I can stay wandering through
the dream where he's close to me.
I try to walk by his side with my
head high and hope he'll stay here
with me, So then I won't be...
Sad and lonely.

Also, here's a picture of my guiding with Matt and my younger brother high-siding at Tight Squeeze Rapid. I put it in here to help you get a scene in your head. Please return it before the semester's over, I don't have any copies. Thanks.

Chance encloses his essay on rafting, which is too long to include here. Anneli returns Chance's compliments:

Chance,

I love your writing! When I read the first piece you wrote it didn't take me any time to get into it and get a feel for it, ya know, kinda like when you know the person writing! It seems like every word fits together perfectly! Your writings are better than some books I've read.

When I finished reading "My First Time" I felt a bit of relief! You really painted a picture for me, "a violent explosion of water" that reminds me of when I went tubing down the St. Joe. I know it doesn't compare to your adventure, but I was ten at the time and to a little girl a small splash seemed like a wall of water towering over my head. Both of your essays tell a lot about you and what your personality is like.

I bet you have millions of stories to send me about everything that's ever happened to you. Which makes me ask myself why I agreed to do this. It's not that I don't like to write but I don't have any completed work to give you, all I have are poems so I guess I'll just have to bore you for now. So don't be mad at me—just tell me you like them anyway!

I wrote my last poem about my boyfriend that was — and is—living in Seattle. It's a long story so I won't go into it.

Yeah, football is a great sport, it's always been one of my favorites. We've played two games and I play outside and inside linebackers and off-line guard. I like linebacker a lot more because you get more of a chance to hit. I got the first and only score of our first game. My next game is on Wed. The 12th at 4:00 at the Jr. High. If you wanta come my number is 63. I'm starting on off-line and I'm really proud of myself for being better than half the guys. So even though I don't really know you I'd like it if you came.

This summer I wrote a lot of poems about a lot of different things so I'm just going to give you a few of them. Talk to you soon,

Anneli

Chance does go to Anneli's football game, and Anneli writes:

I am really flattered that you like my poems. It means a lot to me when somebody likes the one thing I love to do. I also want to thank you for coming to my game. You should have stayed. It turned out to be a great game. We went into triple overtime. Even though we lost, we played a great game as a team.

Chance's and Anneli's love of sports and adventure and their admiration for each others' writing make their partnership successful. Chance boosts Anneli's confidence in her poetry and she, in turn, encourages him. She writes, "I would really like it if you would write me a poem, and I don't care if it starts 'Jack and Jill!' I'll be able to find the greatness in your writing 'cause I know it's gotta be in there." And although Chance never sends Anneli a poem specifically for her, he does share with her a poem he and some friends had written in high school, much to Anneli's delight.

By a sort of modeling, the senior writers can encourage their partners not only to examine their writing strategies and reading responses more closely, but also to ask more detailed questions about their own work with an eye to revision. Some younger partners are surprised to learn that older writers revise, and even ask them for feedback! "Are my descriptions of him good enough for you to form a picture of him? Can you follow my thoughts through the story, or do you find yourself having to go back to reread things?" Queries such as these help younger writers formulate articulate questions of their own, and encourage them to request more from their partners than "do you like it?" or "tell me what you think?"

> I am sending you a poem of mine about my dog who died in October. I had trouble with the last line of the third group. The one that says "but I will accept her death." I don't feel that it fits with the rest so please tell me what you think. If you have another line that would fit there, please tell me. Hope you enjoy it!
>
> LIFE WILL GO ON
>
> I knew it was coming,
> any day now.
> I would wake up to her whimpers
> and see her lie there,
> not even able to move.
>
> But why so soon?
> She was just a puppy,
> not even lived half her life,
> but already had back problems.
> Maybe she needed to go.
>
> It's different without her.
> Nobody to feed my bread crust to,
> nobody to play with.
> I will miss Taffy,
> but I will accept her death.
>
> Life will go on.
>
> Emy

When a young writer knows that the senior partner likes and respects his work, and views his partner as someone whose experience as a writer he values, he is more responsive to his partners' suggestions and even willing to revise. Allen's response to Ken's advice that he "skip the one-sentence questions" (Chapter 3) was to take it: "Anyway, I'm sending 'The Window' with those revisions you suggested. You're right—taking out the 'Oh?s' and 'What?s' makes a big difference." Not many partners have the time in one semester to rewrite, partly, I think, because they are constantly producing new writing for their English classes, and they revise only for publication or for a grade. The two-week turnaround, as Susan Hodgin points out (Chapter 3), means that by the time students get the feedback from their partners, the piece has been turned in to the teacher. Students do, however, rework their writing for the anthology and sometimes for their final portfolios in English, so partners' advice is not in vain.

When writers like and trust each other, they can enjoy collaborating, which is sometimes a new experience for partners. Several partners in our project have shared in the creation of a poem or story. One pair, Tammi and Lolly, did both. Lolly's part is in italics.

THE SWING

I look around the playground to make sure no one else wants the swing.
Luckily, no one does.
I approach the swing and grasp the metal chain in my hand.
The metal is cold to the touch, but I know the sturdy links will support me.
The rubber seat cradles me, and offers up the chance to soar to the sky.
I push off from the earth and let myself go.
Faster and faster I fly, with the supporting arm of the chain in my hand.
I feel as though I could touch the stars.
Then gradually, the swing slows and I see a playground with children.
A breeze brushes past my face, and in the distance I hear a bell.
I realize that my time on the swing is done now, and I get off the comforting cradle of the seat.
As I walk inside, I think of the amazing swing and I hope that we will soon fly again.

Collaboration can be difficult if the partners have definite ideas about where a story should go. One semester, two writers abandoned their elaborate and long collaborative story midway through because neither writer liked what the other was doing with the characters and plot; the experiment almost destroyed their partnership until the senior partner wisely suggested they each write their own story.

A Teacher's View

Excitement about writing, confidence with sharing writing, a greater ability to read and edit, and a sense of community, cited by the young writers themselves as benefits of having a partner, are also noticed by Susan, the teacher of the majority of our project's young writers:

> When the program is followed as designed, my students gain so much from forming a writing friendship. . . . Having a reader relaxes them about their writing, helping them to grow accustomed to hearing someone else besides their English teacher comment about their writing, building a non-threatening audience for them. These partners glean so much and really look forward to the program's culminating project, the anthology of collected writings from each semester's participants; they also look forward to meeting their partner at the closing reception and enjoying everyone's readings, a celebration of publishing their shared and mentored writing.
>
> For those students who have an understanding of commitment, the program works best. I know I am more concerned about my own writing when I have someone waiting to read it. I become more concerned about deadlines and about audience. And more importantly, I become more concerned about feedback: what was my reader's overall impression? Is this work finished? Where should I focus for revision . . . and maybe even how? These become answered questions for most writing partners. Admittedly, some of my students grow disappointed with their partners and return their writing with too little response. Even though my students enjoy the exchange and the reader's response, they often want more than just a reader's response; they want editing. But not every partner is a good reader or editor. Those are learned skills—and something that improves for all program participants. Again, both Candy [Gillis] and I remind our students who has ownership, and we sometimes become the arbitrator for our students. And that's great because it demonstrates our students' trust and gets us involved in their writing partnership. That's what the entire program is about, community—a community working together.

Rewards for Community Writers

What do the older writers gain from having a younger partner? The college students report that they learn much about adolescents and the kinds of things they like to write. They also appreciate the chance to practice responding to writing and to see how young readers view their work:

I thought the experience was valuable because I got a chance to sample the kind of writing going on at a middle school/secondary setting, a grade level I may be teaching down the road. I also got to hone my "positive" response abilities. . . .

[Having a partner] helped me remember what it's like and how it feels to be in the seventh grade. It was nice to have a critic who was basing her suggestions on how she felt and not on how other people told her to feel.

I enjoyed having someone to discuss my writing with and I like to read someone else's writing "just because," not to grade it.

I think it was really good to have the opportunity to read students' writing. It was fun yet educational. It was also a great way to get used to sharing your writing with students. Although it is difficult, I think it is very helpful in establishing a good relationship with students.

I gained respect for a younger person's writing, thoughts, and emotions. Writing is such a personal thing and I was flattered to have had the chance to share writing with junior high and high school students. I also learned to look at a piece of writing objectively without having to criticize unless it was asked of me.

Community writers not in college share many of these reactions. For only a few, the partnerships are not all they expected. One said, "I didn't feel that our exchanges were particularly productive—perhaps I expected more from a high school student than was reasonable. . . ." Overall, writers' comments on their end-semester evaluations (in response to the letter shown in Chapter 4) are positive. Writers enjoy interacting with a young writer and responding to writing in a nonjudgmental way: "I like reading my partner's work. Responding to it is fun since I don't have to grade it." And some people discover that their partnerships support and enrich their own work as writers.

It forced me to write some things I wouldn't have otherwise written. In the end, I valued that.

[Having a partner] gives me an opportunity to get feedback from an entirely different audience. It also encourages me to explore a different type of writing (vs. my job).

The program has caused me to do my own writing but it has also made me realize the poetry and short fiction I write for fun is not appropriate for all audiences.

I am startled by my own openness to an anonymous person and my willingness to submit pieces that are not "happy." And I was startled to receive same from Missy. I thought we'd both be "writing for an audience" but I don't think we are; I think we are writing for ourselves.

Writing partnerships have the potential to build and strengthen a sense of community. As one writer wrote, "I like [the project] and would continue to participate for several reasons: the opportunity to encourage a young writer [and] to 'meet' another young person outside the roles of adult, or parent, or teacher, or teen—as writer to writer; continued, increasing interaction among the many segments of our community can only benefit us all in the long run." Partnerships help people grow as writers and neighbors. The writer who is caused to reflect on her own childhood, to recapture the drama of adolescence now outgrown, or to share a young person's exhuberance has a greater connection to a community's youth. "I got a bit of insight," one writer said, "as to what upper elementary girls are interested in. I glimpsed their fears, for the most part. I remembered some of the old concerns that I used to have—the ones that 'go away' as you grow (like fear of escaped killers, being alone, etc.)." Another wrote, "I gained hope for the writers of tomorrow, both from my partner and the reception. I learned about youth. I received a small glimpse into a world I'm sorely out of touch with—children/teenagers." And how can we as a society not gain by these discoveries?

SHE IS

She is an optimistic teenager living in a battle zone.
She wonders why the shooting never stops.
She hears the thunder of the .38, the shattering clang of the
        breaking glass, the victim's screams, and the
        screeching of the tires as the assailants get away . . .
        once again.
She sees the all too familiar yellow tape fencing the sidewalk
        what seems like everyday.
She wants to be away from it all—free from the hurt and the
        pain.
She is an optimistic teenager living in a battle zone.

She prays that the awe of "Ghetto Star" and "O.G." status
        will never draw her or her brothers and sisters in.
She feels the cold and eerie emptiness come over her as yet
        another close friend is buried
She listens to her grandparents talk of the "good old days,"
        and wonders what happened to them, where they went,
        and whether they ever even existed.
She worries about whether or not, someday, she too will
        have sweet stories to tell her grandchildren when they
        ask *her* what things used to be like.

She cries herself to sleep at night—hoping that tomorrow
    will be better.
She is an optimistic teenager living in a battle zone

She understands that it can all change—even though
    sometimes it seems as if it may never change
She says that things shouldn't be that way—that "soon, it'll
    be different."
She dreams of a world without drug dealers or junkies.
She tries to stay strong.
She hopes that she'll always *be* strong.
She is an optimistic teenager living in a battle zone.

She wonders what she did wrong—what she could have done
    to stop it.
Yet she knows the answer . . . "nothing."
She hates those ignorant people who hide behind false words
    and phrases like "truce" and "it's their own fault"
Yet she knows that she shouldn't hate them—"hate" is what
    got everybody into this whole mess in the first place.
They just don't understand—they *refuse* to understand.
She pretends that it doesn't exist—that everything's
    perfectly alright.
Yet, she knows that it's far from alright or normal. It's all
    just gotten too real—out of control like a giant
    snowball rolling down a hill

You may ask: "who is she?" and "what does she have to do
    with me?"
The truth?
She is the leftovers—an outcast of society. Innocent.
Say what?
Yeah, you heard me. She shouldn't have to escape to the
    suburbs to experience peace, and it shouldn't make a
    difference whether she lives in Bel Air or Compton.
But it does.
And she has everything to do with you . . .

                                    She is our future.

Angela

6

A "Poet Laureate"
and a Poet-in-the-Making

"To Achieve We Must First Attempt" reads the back of my favorite T-shirt. Above the caption are three goggled swimmers, each frozen midstroke, on their ways to personal bests, place finishes, national times. . . . I bought the shirt at one of my son's swim meets and wear it regularly to exercise class to remind me that, if I want to lose those inches and tone those muscles, I have to do much more than what I do easily and regularly. This message applies to writing, too. As writers we tend to stick to what we do best, particularly when we know we must give our writing to someone else. I like to think that our impulse to write in styles and on subjects that seem familiar is not out of laziness but reflects a natural tendency to conserve. Like a river, our words seek a course of maximum power and minimum resistance, so we take risks reluctantly. Less experienced writers especially may not want to move outside secure boundaries, particularly when their audience is unknown. "I'm no good at poetry so I never write it." "I can't write rhymes." "My best writing is true-life stories." Most young writing partners prefer initially to share with their partners writing that has been successful in the past—earned high grades from teachers or high praise from peers. But without risk, growth does not occur. As with other endeavors in life, we do not find our angle of repose without falling downhill. Therefore, it is crucial for writers to push beyond their safe borders, experiment, perhaps produce a work that doesn't.

Encouraging younger writers to step outside the familiar is something I wish all older writing partners would do. By trying new forms themselves, and by sharing writing that is in process, experienced authors not only can help their partners be receptive to suggestions for revision, as I mentioned in Chapter 5, but also can give them the courage to reach beyond comfortable boundaries. The exchange between Ron McFarland and Joe Burnett illustrates the kind of risk-taking and resulting growth that happens when the senior partner becomes a true mentor.

Ron McFarland is a poet, author, and professor at the University of Idaho, where he teaches courses in seventeenth-century and modern poetry, contemporary northwest writers, and creative writing. In 1984 he was named the state's first Writer-in-Residence, a two-year appointment that replaced the position of "state poet laureate." His most recent collection of poems is *The Haunting Familiarity of Things* (1993), and his most recent book *The World of David Wagoner* (1996). His partner, Joe Burnett, is, at the time of their partnership, a ninth-grader, in his second year with the Writing Partners Project. According to his teacher, Joe never wrote poetry until the eighth grade, when a class unit on poetry inspired a love of writing verse. His new-found love led him to join the staff of the literary magazine, and he became poetry editor. In the course of their partnership, which lasts for two consecutive semesters, Ron takes on the role of writing coach, a role Joe welcomes.

Ron is an exceptional mentor, and few partners are as knowledgeable about or so articulate about the nature and history of a genre. In the letters and writing reprinted here, Ron makes clear what he likes and doesn't like in poetry and why. He encourages Joe to abandon his rhymed couplets (witty and clever though they are) and aim for crisp images, concrete detail, and unrhymed verse. By analyzing closely his own and Joe's writing, Ron shows how poetry comes to have meaning and the need for poets to choose their words carefully and to scrutinize their lines; he encourages Joe to examine his own work with a critical eye and ear. He treats Joe as a fellow author, sharing works of his own that are tentative and unpublished, and solicits Joe's advice. And he responds to Joe's work honestly and constructively; when he praises, the praise is sincere. Through an exercise in collaborative writing, Ron guides Joe toward a new way of envisioning and creating poetry. He gives Joe much to digest. As you will see, the partnership is an adventure for both. (Note: I have included in this chapter the nearly complete texts of Ron's letters during the first semester of his partnership. They contain a wealth of information and advice for teachers of poetry and for poets of any age.)

8 September

Dear Writing Partner:

When I was your age, somewhere between 12 and 16 I assume, I was delivering the hometown newspaper (it just came out a couple afternoons a week, so it wasn't much of a bother), playing mediocre trumpet in the band, and trying to figure how I could gain twenty pounds so my parents would let me try out for football. That's how I remember it. Whatever it was I was doing back then, it certainly was not writing, and I would have been stunned to think that one day I would come to regard of myself, at least in a small way, as a writer.

As it turns out, I don't have many regrets about those days. I was pretty active in Boy Scouts at the time, and in that town and in those days being in Boy Scouts was "cool." I guess the only thing I regret is that I didn't gain those twenty pounds, so I did not go out for football. On the other hand, maybe that saved me from a few broken bones, thus leaving them for me to break many years later when I got into soccer, which is one of my on-going passions.

But I do wish I had "gotten into" writing sooner than I did. Every now and then I read a story, poem, or essay by one of my students who is maybe just 18 or 19, and I find myself wishing I could have written that well when I was their age. The fact is I just didn't do much writing when I was in junior high or high school, so when I got to college I had a lot to discover about it, and I'm not sure I've ever caught up.

At any rate, I'm looking forward to communicating with you as your writing partner. I write all sorts of things—poems, short stories, non-fiction. If you have any preferences, let me know and I'll try to send you the sort of writing you want to read. I don't want to dump a big load of the stuff on you, though, so I'll start with a little story and a couple poems.

I look forward to hearing from you.

Sincerely,
Ron McFarland

FISHING THE LAST LIGHT

At Cut Bank Creek last August trout
were biting better than yellowjackets,
rising to Coachmen, Gnats, to anything
showing a red flash. My cut-rate
Taiwan flies unspun themselves
on rocks, on serviceberry, on warm air
stirred to fury in my flailing
desperation for the cut-throat.

Alone I crossed that stream
so happy in my empty-headed glee
I hardly noticed when the sun
began to change its mind and the buzz
of bees and yellowjackets faded
in favor of mosquitoes whining for blood.
Looking up the creek I saw
what every fisherman fears most,
another angler, rod in hand,

creel heavy at his waist, wearing a weathered vest and red
crushed hat, and worst of all
a blissful grin.

I tried to smile, lined up my best
pattern of lies to cast
before his question, "Any luck?"
I said a few. I said just little ones,
a couple good ones, thinking of the hole,
the splash, my Royal Coachman
snagged in its jaw like something
caught in its teeth, thinking how long
it takes a rainbow to forget.

"Around the next bend," he said,
"you'll find a logjam. You can't
miss there. Try anything with red."
I tried to be nice, be grateful,
nodded, thinking of that blasted hole
he'd find behind me, around another bend.
I saw him slapping it to bits.
I saw my rainbow
dancing to his hand and nestled
in his creel, and then in his frying pan.

"Just one thing, though," he said,
"I saw some cougar tracks,
a big one, fresh. They're active
after dark especially." He winked.
I tried to think of what to do,
and seeing clearly in the mind's eye
how that old cat would slip
silent from behind those dark gray logs,
I tried to thank him.
"That hole around the bend,"
I cried out under the rising moon,
"you shouldn't waste your time!"

Dear Mr. McFarland,

Thank you for your material. I enjoyed it. I'm looking forward to hearing from you with more poetry. I like to write poetry. I hope you can
help me improve. Here is a poem I wrote a little while back before my
birthday.

    Sincerely,
    Joe Burnett

FIGURE 6–1

Dear Mr. McFarland

Thankyou for your material I enjoyed it. I'm looking
forward to hearing from you with more poetry. I like to
write poetry. I hope you can help me improve.
Here is a poem I wrote a little while back before
my birthday.

Sincerely,

Joe Burnett
JOE BURNETT

```
              THE BIG STEP UP


Tommorow is my birthday, I've been waiting since my last,
I turn fifteen tomorrow, another year has passed.


I shouldn't be excited, I'll have to be mature,
After all I'm fourteen, that's old enough I'm sure.


Then why am I so tired? I stayed up all the night.
Waiting for your birthday, is half the whole delight.


The presents, they're all great, the food is still all right,
But the part that has you up in chills, is the wait the former night.
```

THE BIG STEP UP

Tomorrow is my birthday, I've been waiting since my last,
I turn fifteen tomorrow, another year has passed.

I shouldn't be excited, I'll have to be mature,
After all I'm fourteen, that's old enough I'm sure.

Then why am I so tired? I stayed up all night.
Waiting for your birthday, is half the whole delight.

The presents, they're all great, the food is still all right,
But the part that has you up in chills, is the wait the former night.

Dear Joe—

Thanks for the poem . . . What struck me most about "The Big Step Up"
is your control of meter. It seems to me that's sort of where I started with
poetry, and I still believe in it, even though I do not write much accentual-syllabic verse. What I mean is that I still believe (Latin, "credo"—
"I believe"—my creed, if you will) in the pulse of the line. I think I
could write it on my tombstone: "Here Lies Ron McFarland: He Believed in the Pulse of the Line." Actually, the *basic* definition of poetry
is "line"; that is, composition by "verse" (the turn of the line) rather
than by sentence. But enough o' that.

I'm enclosing a couple of my more recent (presently unpublished) efforts, so they're still "in progress." That is, they may go through another
revision or two before they eventually see print, *or* I might decide in another month or two that they're destined for the wastebasket. I'll have to
admit that I'm not very defensive of my writing. Occasionally I'll feel very
strongly about one piece or another, but I don't want to make a big deal of
it with someone, because in a few more days I may turn against it myself.

I don't know what you'd like from me in the way of comment on your
work, but before I'd say anything at all I'd want to see several poems
(not just one or two). This definitely includes work "in progress" and
what I refer to sometimes as "inspired fragments," those lines or phrases
(images, whatever) that aren't quite there and maybe never will be.

What if I gave you a line, and then you wrote the next line or two,
and then I wrote the next, and so on (just to see what happened)? I'll
offer a line, and if you want to go with it, fine. Well, in fact, I think you
should "go with it." Also, though, you should send me a line, and I
should have to go with it. That way we would have two poems working
back and forth. Let's try it anyhow. Here's my line: *A single magpie rises
from the road.* Well, I hope you can go somewhere from there!

By the way, we can be on a first-name basis if you'd like. I look forward to hearing from you.

Ron

Joe—

Depending on what I send to you, I'll probably ask different sorts of questions, but I think a good place to start is to ask you (as I often ask myself) "where is this poem really good? where is it not so hot?" I mean I figure there's no way any typical poem is going to be uniformly terrific throughout, so what I want to know is where I've had my best moment, and where I've had my worst. Then I can decide for myself whether to let the worst stand. Maybe I'll *have* to for one reason or another. On the other hand, maybe I should try to do more in the poem of what I'm doing when I'm writing what someone else thinks is my best. [Ron sends two poems, including the one following.]

THE APOLOGY

That night the moon was orange
from the smoke of forest fires,
or almost gold, he had to say,
something thick with value
in exchange for what he knew
he should have said, or rather
what he shouldn't have shouted
a couple hours before.

Now in the half-moon dark
his father stood beside him
awaiting the apology
he couldn't say at night any more
than in broad daylight.
So the words gathered and the moon
drifted in the smoke between them.

Now his father would have to say
something about how long the summer was,
how dry, about the early harvest,
low wheat prices once again,
about the baseball strike, or
anything else to set the world right.

Ron,

I am sending you quite a few of my poems. Not all of them are final quality but they're presentable. I would have sent you more poems before but I was short on time. As for the poem you started, I continued for a few stanzas. I like the idea of a two person poem.

A single magpie rises from the road,
I raise the rifle, just the way my father showed.

FIGURE 6–2

Ron,

I am sending you quite a few of my poems.
Not all of them are final quality but their
presentable. I would have sent you more poems
before but I was short on time. As for
the poem you started, I continued for a few
stanzas. I like this idea of a two person poem.

A single magpie rises from the road,
I raise the rifle, just the way my father showed.

The shot rang out, but just too low,
Relived, I watch the magpie go.

I don't mind no birds today,
If I hit one, great, if not, okay.

If you want a line to write a poem from I can
give you one, but why not a few? Give one a whack.

1) There's nothing like a carpet on tired, worn old feet.
2) Caught in the bright head lights the deer stood frozen.
3) Flying to and fro, the kite dove and spun.
4) Poping up infront of me the rabbit leapt away.

I liked the poem "The Apology". The images are nice and
I like the way you don't really tell what the fight was
about because it's not that important. However I'm not
sure about the last stanza. I haven't ever really tryed
writting poems that don't rhyme, so I don't have
much input to make it sound better. I hope you can help
me write some non-rhyming material. I'm not really sure.

The shot rang out, but just too low,
Relieved, I watch the magpie go.

I don't mind no birds today,
If I hit one, great, if not, okay.

If you want a line to write a poem from I can give you one, but why
not a few? Give it a whack.

1) There's nothing like a carpet on tired, worn old feet.
2) Caught in the bright head lights the deer stood frozen.
3) Flying to and fro, the kite dove and spun.
4) Popping up in front of me the rabbit leapt away.

I liked the poem "The Apology." The images are nice and I like the
way you don't really tell what the fight was about because it's not that
important. However I'm not sure about the last stanza. I haven't ever
really tried writing poems that don't rhyme, so I don't have much input
to make it sound better. I hope you can help me write some non-rhyming material. I'm not really sure. . . . [Joe attaches several poems, including the two below.]

THE DEAD TOAD ON THE ROAD

The moonlight spread from coast to coast,
blotting out the starry host.
A gentle breeze to calm the mind,
whispering, calling from behind.
The roadway had nothing to hide,
no cars had chosen upon it to ride.
No better time to cross the road.
Confidence swelled within the toad.
But, alas, the toad would find,
he looked ahead but not behind.
A common mistake among the toad,
not both ways to look upon the road.
A heavy cement truck that night was coming,
its powerful engine deeply thrumming,
Onward it went without a care,
of the poor toad which was lying there.
The toad was reduced to its simple components,
no pain, no brain, and a few bone fragments.
The truck just continued, the driver unaware,
of the road kill behind him, on the road there.

WAITING

I've waited forever, he's not going to come.
Sitting alone, outside in the sun.

He promised he'd be there, but where is he now?
Why does he do this, why and how?

How can he not know how he hurts me?
How can he be blind, why can't he see

That I can't go on? He does this too much.
He should support me, not just be a crutch.

I don't want to lose him, but he chose this end.
He's less of a dad, and more just a friend.

10-20

Dear Joe:

Thanks for sending a good number of your poems so that I could get a more complete sense of "where you are" in the craft (or sullen art, as Dylan Thomas suggested) of writing poems. You're at an interesting stage, I'm inclined to say (having been there once), maybe at a crossroads.

Reading your good efforts, I find myself wanting to have an influence on you, to have some effect or impact—even if it turns out to be a collision. Someday I may send you my lengthy essay entitled "A Rambling Discourse about Poetry," but I don't want to burden you with it just now. I do, however, want to say a couple things about the immediate constituents (lowest common denominators, if you like) of poetry.

1. It is sonic.
2. It is rhythmic.

The corollary to Theorem #1 (to sustain my mathematical metaphor—I've always been awful at math), is that while poems may rhyme, they do not have to; that is, rhyme is *not* an immediate constituent of poetry. After perhaps centuries of "living" as oral poems, Homer's *Iliad* and *Odyssey* were first written down around 800 BC, and along with the Golden Age poetry of 5th century BC Greece (the odes of Pindar, the lyrics of Sappho, the dramatic poetry of Sophocles and others) *none* of it rhymed. The great Latin poems of Rome's Golden Age, around the first century AD (the works of Virgil, Horace, Ovid, Catullus, Martial), did *not* rhyme. Rhyme does not become important in poetry till around 1100 (the Anglo-Saxon poem, *Beowulf*, does not rhyme). Much famous poetry (Milton's *Paradise Lost,* for example) does not rhyme, but of course the first major challenge to rhyme was Whitman's *Leaves of Grass*, about 1855. By 1925 (roughly) rhyme was more "the exception" than "the rule."

All of this is *not* to say that what we think of as "modern" or "contemporary" poems may not rhyme or (more importantly) that the mod. or contemp. poet has no obligation when it comes to how the poem sounds, whether it strikes the ear, etc. I'd say, in fact, that the burden is greater than ever when it comes to the sonic obligations of poets today. We are expected to be more subtle, less obvious, than ever before. We rely more on alliteration and assonance for our music, and if we do choose to rhyme occasionally, we are expected to be much more sophisticated than those who came before us (and it's pretty hard to be more sophisticated than poets like Longfellow, Keats, Emily Dickinson). Dickinson exploited the so-called "slant" or "near" rhyme (so that in its place "gone" and "tune" more-or-less rhyme). Consider this passage:

> There is no one <u>haw</u>king oranges
> In the street an <u>auto-rickshaw</u> choking
> Towards the <u>ho</u>spital

What makes this "free verse" is not just the lack of rhyme, of course, but the lack of meter (measure, or rhythmic regularity). I've underlined the key sounds in the passage—assonance—vowels that sound alike (and often are spelled quite differently in good old non-phonetic English). This is a *very* musical tercet, and the ear hears it easily when the lines are read aloud, but the sounds are subtle. The poet does not beat us over the head with them. And the sounds (unlike end rhymes) are not predictable.

Okay, so let's say that's Lesson #1: That poems can be rich in sound without rhyming, and that in the process they usually gain in power because the sonics are more subtle.

The second lesson concerns rhythm. The theory of free verse poetry is that line, by its very nature (just like language by its very nature) is "rhythmic." The line does *not* have to go

> ba-bump,
> ba-bump

in order to be rhythmic. Again, the mod/contemp poet is after subtlety. Consider the following sentences (prose): "The shotgun hung inside on the porch, right over the front door. The old man always kept it loaded." Now suppose you create lines:

> The shotgun hung inside
> on the porch, right over
> the front door. The old man
> always kept it loaded.

Well, suddenly it becomes poetry (we won't argue whether it's good or bad!). When those prose sentences are set up as *lines,* they acquire a rhythm, a pulse. The weight, feel, beat of these lines is vastly different from this:

> The shotgun hung inside on the porch,
> right over the front door.
> The old man always kept it loaded.

And the pulse there is very different from this:

The shotgun hung
inside on the porch,
right
over the front door.
the old man
always kept it
loaded.

And that varies from this:

The shotgun hung
inside
on the porch,
right over the front door.
The old
man
always
kept it loaded.

Okay now, there are 4 versions of the same "stanza" of the "poem." Which is better? Why? Now the *important* thing about questions like those is not "which answer is right," but how we go about trying to find out. The 1st version is the most "regular." It is cast in what is known as "syllabic" form, a very subtle line for poems in English, because our "meter" is accentual-syllabic (involves both accents and syllables). The "form" of #1 is the 6 syllable line (count 'em up). If form means a lot to you, and I suspect it does, I'd think you would gravitate toward version #1.

But then because it adheres to syllabic guidelines, #1 involves pretty odd (even "forced" or "unnatural") line breaks, whereas #2 breaks at natural syntactic (sentence) places. The fact that each line is end-stopped (period or comma) is a sign of that, though you could be a "syntactic" or "grammatical" free-verse poet without punctuating the end of *every* line.

The 3rd version might appeal to a true free-wheeler. If you read it properly, with due attention to the line breaks, you will see how the rhythm is. Lines like "right" and "loaded" *are* lines, after all, and must be read as such. As one-word lines, though, they call extra attention to themselves, and the wise poet is thinking exactly that thought when he sets up such lines.

Of course that 4th version is pretty wild, too. It plays on the page because the poet has used a drop-line technique. Inevitably (note the word!), this version has special visual impact that the others do not. Reading it aloud, you won't "hear" what the poet has written, but poems are *also* intended (usually—nowadays at any rate) to be *seen* as well as to be heard. Of course I'd say there's no purpose at all in writing version #4 if you don't intend for someone to read the poem.

Ultimately, I think poetry comes down to what we do with the language—more with how we say it than with what we have to say (fortunately, at least for me). So I always encourage would-be poets to become wordwise, which means to acquire a vocabulary, of course, but also to develop a sensitivity to the sounds of words and to their heft, and to how they rattle against each other, how they string together rhythmically. But enough o' that.

Among your poems I liked "The Dead Toad on the Road" best. I think your couplet form fits well with that sort of playful subject and I can see how it could be shaped up a little. Heck, I feel sort of inclined to take a shot at it myself. I'll think about it. "Waiting" is a poem that says something of genuine worth and feeling, but I'd say the form is all wrong for it. I would like to see the poem "show" or imply more and tell less (too much telling after the first couplet, I'd say). Understatement, subtlety—this poem could acquire wonderful *power* (I mean impact, velocity—it could be .357 mag instead of .22, if you know what I mean). Build from images. "Sitting alone in the sun . . . ." Then what? Don't tell me "I'm waiting for Dad" or "he said he'd be here, but he isn't." Instead, give me another image, something concrete and tangible. It could be the rustle of leaves or a piece of wadded notebook paper, maybe the torn strips of a love note someone passed in class. Do you see what I'm getting at?

Now, as to the poem I started, what I had in mind was that you'd write a line or two, then me, then you, etc. A collaborative effort. Okay?

But let's take a look at the meter in your opening couplet, because it doesn't quite work if you examine it closely, and if you're going to write that sort of poem, you *do* have to examine it closely!

/ = stressed
u = unstressed

> u /u /u /u / u /
> A single magpie rises, from the road.

> u / u / u / u / u /u   /
> I raise my rifle, just the way my father showed.

I guess you'd be a little suspicious about the meter just because that second line is so much longer than the first. Technically, the first line has 10 syllables and is pretty regular iambic pentameter, while the second has 12 syllables and is iambic hexameter. (By the way, your next couplet is written in iambic tetrameter—lines of 8 syllables.)

So the form breaks down. But suppose I revise this just a bit. If you're going to shoot the bird, let's make it a pheasant, and you'll probably go after it with a shotgun:

> A pheasant rises from the road.
> I raise my gun the way Dad showed.

The shot rings out, but strikes too low.
Relieved, I watch the pheasant go.

Maybe we could take it from there? But if you do go back to this poem, stick with the tetrameter line and build on it some. Follow the flight of the pheasant. Okay? The famous poet Wallace Stevens wrote, "Poetry is a pheasant disappearing in the brush." Interesting notion, eh?

Okay, here's a start from the lines you offered me, and I'd like you to build the poem by a line or two, but (a) without using rhyme and (b) without trying to impose meter.

Caught in his headlights the deer froze.
Ed had drunk just enough beer that night
at the Corner Club, just enough to

The first word you write to develop the thought I've left dangling must appear on the *next* line (not right after "to"). Note a couple things about where we've started here. One, we've got a bit of a story under-way, which is nice. Two, we have a character (by name), and we've even named a local bar. The poet always needs to stick to the concrete—avoid flatness, abstractions. Don't even be satisfied with "the bar" when you can name it. Should I have said "beer" or "Budweiser"? What do you think? I used "beer" because it could play off (in subtle, internal rhyme) against "deer," but maybe I shouldn't have. Three, the repetition of the phrase "just enough" adds a little rhythm and emphasis as well, which is nice as long as we don't get carried away. I look forward to seeing where you go "from here" with these two poems. Meanwhile, you asked to see some of my poems that rhyme. I feel a bit odd about sending any, as I'm no great believer in rhyme or its supposed attractions, but I'm sending a few just "for the record."

Ron McFarland

It would be nice to know someone
who liked poetry, to have a friend
who could write the stuff, not rhymes
or what goes ba-boomp, ba-boomp sometimes
like a washing machine, but words that do
strange things even in broad daylight
on an otherwise innocent white page,
words that keep you up all night
weeping, wondering, or in a rage.

Untitled—this one is new—written with what I've been talking about in mind—any ideas for a title?

Ron,

Thank you for all the material you sent me. It took me some time to sort through it but I think I got a lot out of it. Please be patient as this is

FIGURE 6–3

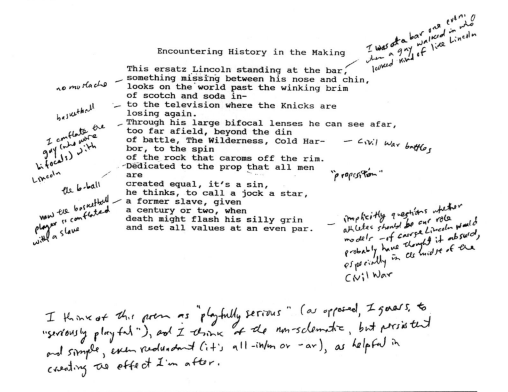

I was at a bar one even' (?)
then a guy walked in who
looked kind of like Lincoln

Encountering History in the Making

This ersatz Lincoln standing at the bar,
— something missing between his nose and chin,
looks on the world past the winking brim
of scotch and soda in-
— to the television where the Knicks are
losing again.
— Through his large bifocal lenses he can see afar,
too far afield, beyond the din
of battle, The Wilderness, Cold Har-
bor, to the spin
of the rock that caroms off the rim.
— Dedicated to the prop that all men
are
created equal, it's a sin,
he thinks, to call a jock a star,
— a former slave, given
a century or two, when
death might flash his silly grin
and set all values at an even par.

no mustache
basketball
I conflate the guy (who wore bifocals) with Lincoln
the b-ball
now the basketball player is conflated with a slave

— Civil War battles
"proposition"

— implicitly questions whether athletes should be our role models — of course Lincoln would probably have thought it absurd, especially in the midst of the Civil War

I think of this poem as "playfully serious" (as opposed, I guess, to "seriously playful"), and I think of the non-schematic, but persistent and simple, even redundant (it's all -in/in or -ar), as helpful in creating the effect I'm after.

confusing sometimes. Here is an effort toward a poem. Please suggest anything because I need to know what I'm doing right and wrong.

Joe

Cold wind blows newly fallen snow
high into drifts out side.
Peering—through frost covered windows
two anxious eyes watch and wait.

A single pair of lights, pierce the darkness
forging a path for one brave soul.
Moving slowly with caution
anxious, eyes follow the beacons.

A single child rushed outside
taking the hand of her hero.

Everything's fine now
Cause Daddy's home.

Caught in his headlights the deer froze
Ed had drunk just enough beer that night
at the Corner Club, just enough to
slow his mind and reflexes.

He saw it coming but couldn't think
couldn't move his feet to the brakes
to avoid it.

(I like the word 'Beer' because Budweiser doesn't really sound as good
to me.)

11-11

Joe—

Yes, yes, yes! This is it. This is the way I think you should be heading
with your poetry. . . .

Actually, it's easier to say what you're doing *right* just now than it is
to say what you're doing "wrong" (if that's even the correct word
here)—and that is good news. Consider your first two lines:

Cold wind blows newly fallen snow
high into drifts outside.

What's wrong here? Nothing, nothing at all. The natural music of
the language (sounds *and* rhythms) is working for you here, and it's
working "naturally." The reader is unaware of any forcing of language
in order to achieve something "Poetickall." I note also that only one
"flat" function word (into—and it is necessary) enters these lines—all
the rest of your language is "significant" (what I call Power-words as
opposed to Function-words, not that you can survive without F-words
[you can, however, survive without *the* F-word], but it's just as well to
keep them to a minimum).

Then the next two lines:

Peering through frost-covered windows
two anxious eyes watch and wait.

Now something "happens," but we (readers, that is) don't know
what, and that's fine, creates a little suspense, but it's more the suspense
of eagerness than of dread, as might have been the case if the eyes were
"nervous" instead of "anxious." The w sounds, appropriate to the wind,
come through well in these lines. In the process of revision, of course,
one *can* (must? should?) ask oneself whether one should have improved
on, say, "covered." What if you'd said "frost-dimmed" or "frost-tinted"?
Or something else.

FIGURE 6–4

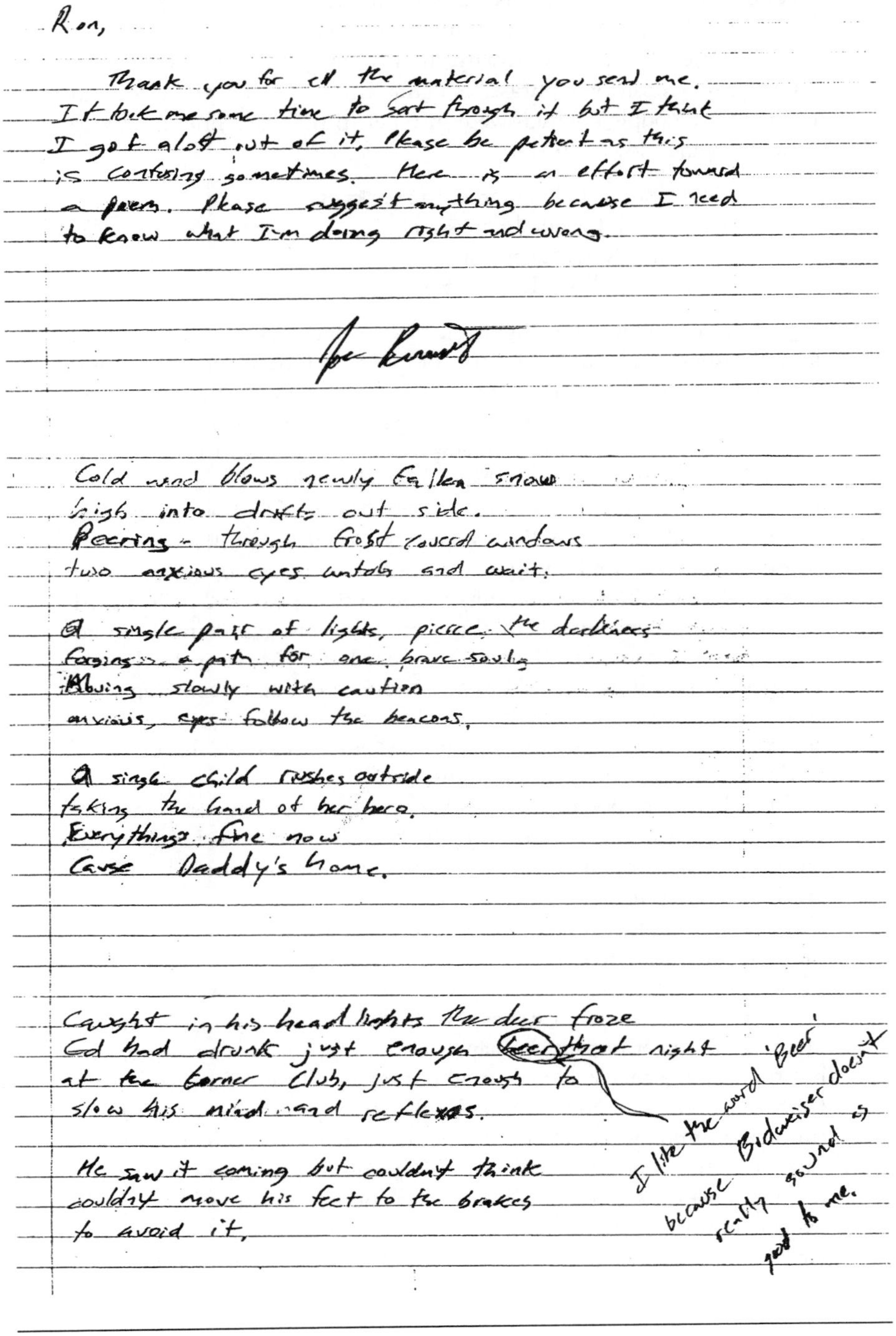

Ron,

Thank you for all the material you send me.
It took me some time to sort through it but I think
I got a lot out of it. Please be patient as this
is confusing sometimes. Here is an effort toward
a poem. Please suggest anything because I need
to know what I'm doing right and wrong.

Joe Everett

Cold wind blows newly fallen snow
high into drifts out side.
Peering through frost covered windows
two anxious eyes untold and wait.

A single pair of lights pierce the darkness
forging a path for one brave soul
moving slowly with caution
anxious eyes follow the beacons.

A single child rushes outside
taking the hand of her hero.
Everything's fine now
Cause Daddy's home.

Caught in his head lights the deer froze
Ed had drunk just enough beer that night
at the corner club, just enough to
slow his mind and reflexes.

He saw it coming but couldn't think
couldn't move his feet to the brakes
to avoid it.

I like the word 'beer'
because Budweiser doesn't
really sound good to me.

Okay, the quatrain form works pretty well here. Let's examine the second quatrain as a whole. Note that I'm cranking in a couple small but essential changes of the sort an editor might feel free to suggest—the verb "pierce" has to agree with the subject "pair," which is singular (the plural prepositional phrase "of lights" threw you off), and it seemed to me that a couple commas were in order in the third line, if only to slow the reader down a little:

A single pair of lights pierces the darkness
forging a path for one brave soul.
Moving slowly, with caution,
anxious eyes follow the beacons.

Why not "A pair of headlights pierces the darkness"? Just thought I'd ask, or rather think out loud. I sort of like the "forging a path" phrase, but I've got mixed emotions about "one brave soul." It just seems too heavy, too "loaded" for the context. (I have to admit at this point that of course I've read the whole poem a couple times, so I know where you're headed, and I'm very conscious of what advice I'm giving about this stanza of the poem because I think you sort of bail out in the last stanza, and I already know I'm going to ask you to re-think it. Already I think I know you well enough to suspect that you, too, are not very comfortable with the last quatrain.) Also in this quatrain I have mixed feelings about "beacons," but that's probably just me. I think I'd go ahead and indicate the character's gender here: "Moving slowly, her anxious eyes / follow . . . ." Now the chore would be to come up with something other than "the beacons" for the revised last line of the stanza. Now, I'm not forgetting about the "one brave soul." It's just that nothing "neat" has come to mind just yet.

I think a lot of poems strike us because the poet has just somehow managed to think of something really "neat" to say. Yes, I realize the word is slangy, but it has a noble origin, coming from the Latin "nitidus," which means "shining or lustrous or bright. . . ."

I'm thinking now that I like the word "caution" and how it sort of picks up the first vowel sound in "follow," so I guess if I were revising (that is, re-seeing) the poem, I'd try to find a place for that word.

Then we get to the last stanza, in which I think you get in too much of a hurry. You get impatient, maybe with the poem, or maybe yourself, but the result is that you blurt it all out: you spill the beans, you "tell" (instead of "show"). Now, it may be that how you revise the previous stanza will influence what you decide to do in the last one, but what I suggest is that you take what Robert Bly calls "a leap" here. Soar over me; jump over the rooftop of your reader's house; say something I don't expect; surprise, stun, amaze me! I'll leave it at that. But *don't* surprise me by "what you say" (e.g., she shot the old fart, her father), but by "how you say it."

I hope this doesn't sound cruel of me, but I'd like to think it is becoming harder for you to write poems now. It *should* be harder to write a
good poem. Or to put it another way, it should be fairly easy to turn out
a jingle, a bit of verse, whatever. By the way, once you get rid of me, you
can always go back to what you were doing before. You're a free agent
in the world, after all! But what I'd like to say right now is that if you
keep at the hard work, it *will* get easier.

Now, let's go to our collaborative poem:

> Caught in his headlights the deer froze.
> Ed had drunk just enough beer that night
> at the Corner Club, just enough to
> slow his mind, to strip the gears
> of his reflexes.
>
> Now he sees it coming but cannot think,
> cannot move his feet to brakes and clutch,
> chokes up. It seems the deer is dancing
> in the road

Okay, I'm stranding you here. I've modified your "reflexes" reference
because slowing his mind and reflexes was too predictable. I wanted to
surprise the reader, something you should *almost* always at least think
about doing. At any rate, you should probably avoid giving what the
reader expects. Anyhow, you'll note that I've shifted verb tense to the
present in the second stanza. As we move toward impact, I want the
reader involved directly in the drama. My only important contribution
to our ongoing poem at this point (I think) is the (I hope "neat") idea
of the deer dancing in the road. What I'd like from you is (1) to complete the line I've started, running it more-or-less as long as the others,
(2) to end the stanza with a short line, and (3) to write just the first
(longish) line of the next stanza.

This is going pretty well, I think, and I look forward to your next
contributions. I hope you can think of something "neat" to do with your
poems as well as with ours.

Meanwhile, I'm enclosing what I think is an interesting example of
revision—first, the poem "Why I Love Baseball" in the short, tight form
in which I initially composed it about two years ago, and second, the
same poem as I revised it about two days ago. Question: Should I have
said "torn" or "tortured" ligaments instead of "twisted"? Question: Was
it a good idea to toss out "my love" at the end (even though it rhymed
rather nicely with "glove")? Question: Am I doing too much "telling"
in the second stanza? Any other "questions," I hope you'll feel free to
ask yourself.

You're making good progress—thanks!

Ron

WHY I LOVE BASEBALL

Working my hand into one of those
four-fingered gloves designed for
second basemen, I wonder why these days
so many people seem to hate baseball.

When I was about eight
my brother had a glove like this,
and a few years down the road
he came back unscathed from Vietnam.

Another brother I know of
apparently tried to field a Cong grenade,
maybe a basket catch like Willie Mays.
I don't know whether he loved the game.

Gloves like this one hold the hand steady,
as if Johnny Antonelli himself were
holding your hand firmly to the dirt
for a hot grounder years before the war.

With an old glove like this and a new baseball,
my love, you could start the whole world over.

WHY I LOVE BASEBALL

Working my hand into one of those stiff
four-fingered gloves designed for
second basemen, I wonder why
even before the strike, so many people
turned against baseball,
favoring the quick kill,
raw meat, cracked bones, and twisted ligaments
of football.

We have become impatient.
We have lost our enthusiasm
for the subtle, the elusive,
the comfort of peanuts and
sunflower seeds and the sweet
boredom of a summer afternoon.

When I was about eight
my brother had a glove like this, a glove
that no amount of neatsfoot oil
could soften.
Nothing could break it in, and when one

golden afternoon he left it stranded on second,
it never returned,
but he came back a few years down the road
unscathed from Vietnam with a story of how he was
left on second with two out and the score tied
when the mortars fell on Pleiku.

Another brother I know of
apparently tried to field a Cong grenade,
maybe a basket catch like Willie Mays.
But I don't know how much he loved the game.

Gloves like this one hold the hand steady,
as if Johnny Antonelli himself
were holding your hand firmly to the dirt
for a hot grounder years before the war.

With an old glove like this and a new baseball,
you could start the whole world over.

To: Ron McFarland
From: Joe

Cold winds blow newly fallen snow,
piling high drifts outside.

Peering through frost filled windows,
two nervous eyes watch and wait.

A piercing pair of headlights shine,
smashing the frozen darkness.

Moving slowly with caution,
her impatient eyes follow its path.

Eyes draw to a halt,
silence ensues as the engine stops rumbling.

Moving quickly from the window,
Mittens and jacket are thrown on.

Hugs are exchanged, as father and daughter,
tramp inside to steaming cups of cocoa.

Caught in his head lights, the deer froze,
Ed had drunk just enough beer that night
at the Corner Club, just enough to
slow his mind, to skip the gears
of his reflexes.

Now he sees it coming but cannot think,
cannot move his feet to the brakes and clutch,
chokes up. It seems the deer is dancing
in the road, asking to be struck
by a drunken driver

Nothing could have prepared Ed for the reeling impact.

Ron,

I'm sorry that this letter is short. It's 11:30 and I'm trying to finish my homework. About "Why I Love Baseball":

I like the "twisted" ligaments as is.

I also like it just a tad better w/o "my love" at the end of the second one.

I hope the revision I've made to my poem are better. I had a bit of trouble thinking about what to add to our poem. But that might just be the fact I'm way over tired.

Thanks much,
Joe

Joe—

Thanks for the good work, particularly on your poem in couplets, which we might title "Waiting" or "Waiting at Night" or "Waiting in the Dark." Something like that. I have only a couple suggestions: 1. convert the passive voice in the 6th couplet to the active ("She throws on jacket and mittens")—and, to do it "right," I'd have her put on the jacket first, as that's how most people do it; 2. convert the passive voice in the last couplet, too, but do something else as well. I'd want to save the cocoa, but maybe surprise the reader somewhere at this point.

Here's my rationale. I think the poet should be a step ahead of the reader—not necessarily a hop, skip, and jump ahead, and not even (necessarily) a mile ahead, although those alternatives are quite possible. But just a step ahead is usually enough. This would mean that the poet has already thought what the reader was thinking and has taken that into consideration. But here's where the poet's special imagination comes into play: he/she does *not* (at least not "necessarily"—in fact, I'd say "rarely") "reward" the reader's expectations. Someone wrote, "No surprise for the writer, no surprise for the reader." Or if they didn't write that, they blamed well should've!

Especially at the end of the poem the poet should be thinking, "I know where you think this is going, but ha!" Something like that. Of course the reason the poet knows where his or her readers are going is that the poet has aimed them in that direction. I'm not saying we should *always* tease the readers' expectations, but it seems that I'm saying we usually should, though of course whether we "tease" or "jolt" is another matter, eh?

Here's your poem (with commentary):

> Cold winds blow newly fallen snow,
> piling high drifts outside.
>
> Peering through frost-filled windows,
> two nervous eyes watch and wait.
>
> A piercing pair of headlights shine,
> <u>smashing</u> the frozen darkness.   *(how about "slicing"? or "carving"?)*
>
> Moving slowly, with caution,
> her impatient eyes follow its path.
>
> Eyes draw to a halt.
> Silence ensues as the engine stops rumbling.
>
> Moving quickly from the window,
> She throws on jacket and mittens.
>
> They hug each other, father and daughter,
> tramp inside to steaming cups of cocoa.

A great deal "goes right" here. You sustain form within the free verse line, and you show a developing awareness of what musicians call a "good ear." As you can see, I've just altered your last couplet to the active voice, but otherwise I haven't messed with it. This has to remain *your* poem.

In that vague sense I often get when working with people on their writing (poetry or prose), I sense that this one is getting to the place where "it is what it's going to be. . . ." Still, some "bright ideas" come to mind with that last couplet:

> They stand by the cooling engine,
> tramp inside to steaming cups of cocoa.

or

> Not touching, they stand a moment in the snow,
> then tramp inside to steaming cups of cocoa.

What I'm suggesting/implying/saying here is to leave a little mystery even at the end of the poem. Why not use that cold/hot contrast, too? I'd say this poem has come along quite well, by the way—good work.

Now, on to our poor deer. I'm going to play a trick on you and bring this one to an end, and then I'm going to try a different "assignment," just for fun.

> Caught in his headlights, the deer froze.
> Ed had drunk just enough beer that night

at the Corner Club, just enough to
slow his mind, to strip the gears
of his reflexes.

Now he sees it coming, but cannot think,
cannot move his feet to the brakes and clutch,
chokes up. It seems the deer is dancing
on the black ice, asking to be struck
by a drunken driver.

Or maybe she only wants to dance a quick
tango, take a turn on the asphalt
ballroom floor, with any drunken sailor
willing to pay the price, one dollar,
whoever he is.   (OR *no matter what happens*)
which?

I "finished" this one because I wanted to illustrate my point about
being a step ahead of the reader. I'd argue that the reader *expects* the
poem to head in the direction of your next line ("Nothing could have
prepared Ed for the reeling impact"), and of course there's nothing
"wrong" with it, but I want you to expand your mind here. If you expand your mind, via your imagination, then you'll expand the reader's
mind. Or so I theorize.

Okay, on to my next scheme. You *must* use at least 3 words from each
of the following lists in your next poem, which must run (let's say) at
least 16 lines. Please note that you may (indeed must—obviously) use
your own words as well; moreover, you may use other words from the
lists, as you prefer. Also, you may alter the form of any given word (for
example, "dream" could be plural—"dreams," or it could be turned into
a past tense verb—"dreamed," or it could become a verbal—"dreaming"). Any qualifier could be seen as an adjective ("careless") or an ad-
verb ("carelessly"). Get it? have fun!

Nouns/Substantives	Verbs	Qualifiers
dream	grab	savage
aspen	play	crazy
home	scatter	careless
Idaho	learn	supple
fox	dissolve	windy
bones	cry	green
despair	smear	sharp
verve	serenade	trivial

Now, to make this game fair, you have to supply me with similar lists, but
maybe with not so many words—say 5 or 6 per column. By the way, I formed
these lists by looking at a few pretty much random contemporary poems by
2 or 3 different poets. I just grabbed what struck my fancy at the time.

I guess we'll have a chance to meet each other December 13. I do hope you'll be there. By the way, just as a matter of curiosity, my son Jon has recently taken to writing poems. I'll have to say I was very surprised, as his life seems to be mostly football, basketball, bikes, skiing, etc. But I was gratified, too. I'm one of those people who think the world would probably be a better place if *everyone* wrote poems, or at least tried to. Or, as an alternative hypothesis, I figure the world wouldn't be any *worse off* if everyone wrote poems occasionally. . . .

WHAT WRITERS KNOW

Certain things we know about
our own work: what came
unbidden, at a moment's notice.
at the drop of a fireman's hat,
as a stitch in the side of time.

We know what struggled to birth
more dead than alive
and caused us no end of pain
and still does when we think about it,
which we try not to do.

We know what never came to life,
what died deep down inside
and cries out from time to time,
whining for our attention.
And we know when to listen.

Ron and Joe's exchange stops temporarily for winter break. Joe submits his poem "Cold Winds" for the anthology in its revised form. During the break, Ron reflects on the first semester's work in this evaluation of the project:

I think the communications with Joe about his poems were probably more valuable for me than they were for him. I found myself trying to explain what I think is important in writing poems, and to justify my long-held beliefs as well. Moreover, I had to "show" it all, to demonstrate how it works, or should work, in my own poems and in his, and I had to at least make an effort to communicate with a boy of just 13 or 14 instead of the usual college sophomore.

I think I/we made progress, and that progress involved weaning Joe away from very conservative, low-risk couplets to free verse. I should point out that the free verse has also been conservative and low-risk, but I think we are getting at the "immediate constituents" or the "lowest common denominators" of poetry. Next semester I think we'll shoot for greater quantity, and I suspect we'll return to meter and rhyme, at least for the sake of exercise.

This is not exactly what happens. After Ron initiates the renewed partnership, Joe writes:

> Dear Ron,
>
> I am sorry for not writing you for a while. I seem to always have something going on.
> I liked your poem. I wasn't able to understand all of it really well. . . .
> I am giving you a poem I wrote recently. I haven't had time to try some more "real poetry." I would like to keep up this style and also do some rewriting of some of my old poems we were talking about.
>
> Later,
> Joe

Despite his expressed interest in continuing to experiment with what he now refers to as "real poetry," Joe sends another verse in couplets, his favorite form. Although Ron is disappointed that Joe is again writing couplets, he respects what he perceives as Joe's preferences. He writes, "So you present a challenge to me here. As a teacher of people who want to write serious poems (or at least think they do), even though their poems may be humorous or witty, I feel obliged to get them headed in the direction I think will get them where they want to be. But arguably, your interests are different, and I can respect that. . . . So here's what I propose. As long as you want to write this sort of thing, I'll help you shape it up as well as I can. . . ."

But then Joe does somewhat of an "about face." First he responds positively, as usual, to Ron's suggestions: "I read your letter carefully. I understand what you're saying about rhythm in the poetry. I think I'll start counting every syllable in the stanzas I write. . . . I also think it might be a good idea to try reading some poetry. I obviously don't do that nearly enough. I would like to continue giving you new stuff. I think I can take your comments and write a poem trying to use your suggestions. . . ." Then he returns to his course of writing less strongly rhymed, less strongly metered verse:

> The sunlight glinting off the snow.
> The long walk home, in sub zero weather,
> As snaky mist, chases the cars,
> I can't help thinking, "how far must I go?"
>
> Numbing my ears, nipping my face,
> biting my fingers, the sub zero weather,
> follows me home, after school.
> I keep myself, at a steady pace.

For his part during the semester, Ron continues his support and encouragement. " Yes! This is the sort of thing I had in mind. First, that you move away from the couplets, and second, that you aim for greater subtlety. You do both very well in this little poem." He continues to provide Joe with detailed explanations of his reactions ("I very much admire the subdued rhyme scheme here (abca). It's just right. . . ."), to illustrate his points with his own and others' poetry, and to suggest "assignments" for Joe to try:

> Find an animal that fits a scene or place. In baseball, for example, the cliché for the late part of the season is "the dog days of August" (hot, and the players are sort of wearing down, falling into slumps). Then set up a poem using details and images of the scene, place, event (whatever). Write this poem in a loose form using random rhyme and variable line length. . . .

Although Joe never completes Ron's "assignments" or sends Ron revisions, Joe obviously grows as a writer because of his willingness to take risks. Never in the semester does he return to comfortable ground. Or perhaps Joe's comfort zone has now widened:

> . . . I wrote this poem at midnight on Tuesday, just before writing partners is due. I like, and enjoy writing this style. Couplets are for losers. . . .

Joe began his partnership "at crossroads" but ends as a more versatile and self-aware writer, moving in new directions. Nor are the rewards of the partnership lost to Ron, who concludes the semester with a more well-defined poetry credo, a better understanding of how much or how little advice to give struggling writers, and a sense that his coaching has made a difference. Perhaps fittingly, Ron's last response to Joe's writing ends on the same note as his first:

> I don't know whether I'd go so far as to say that couplets are for "losers," but what I think is that language is sensitive to time. It can get "dated," and so can the forms we use. . . . This poem looks pretty good to me, but I find myself wanting to work on its pulse (beat, rhythm). . . .

" 'Here Lies Ron McFarland: He Believed in the Pulse of the Line.' "

7

A Partnership Across Generations

Joe would find a kindred spirit in Ralph Zeigler, a community writer who loves verse. Ralph is the oldest partner in my project—eighty-two as I am writing. The self-described "farm hand-construction worker-cabinet maker-business owner-Union representative-millwright and finally retiree" (Chapter 2) has written poetry all his life in response to personal and public events. His partner, Crystal, is in the eighth grade at the time of their partnership. She does not consider herself a poet and prefers writing fiction. Their partnership is an example of how writers can connect across boundaries that separate people by age, interest, and experience. Like other elders who have participated in Writing Partners, Ralph is uncertain, initially, how he and his partner will relate—whether she will like his writing, whether he will be of help to her, if the partnership will be productive. Although a father and grandfather and close to his family, Ralph is aware of the gap between his educational and literary experiences and Crystal's. "[Being a writing partner] is sort of a challenge," he writes at the end of the semester, "for a retired person. Many of us lived in another period, where traditional poetry was predominate. I cross over, but still adhere to rhyming couplets even in blank verse." Their first semester's correspondence (which begins late, in October) shows that despite their preference for different styles of writing and their sixty-six years' difference in age, Ralph and Crystal have quite a bit in common—they appreciate each other's writing, respond with honesty and sensitivity, and, like Joe, take some risks. As you will see, their relationship is very different from Ron's and Joe's and, in some ways, more typical of partnerships.

As their exchange begins, Ralph introduces himself:

Oct. 1

Dear Writing Partner;

This is perhaps a new experience for you and I assure you that it is for me.

I recall when I first became interested in expressing myself in writing. I received special commendation for a report I wrote on Leonardo da Vinci as a fifth grader. Later as an eighth grader I assisted my sister, in high school, on an essay that achieved merit status.

Throughout high school I thoroughly enjoyed writing themes and verse for English and American Literature some times even for my friends. I boasted that I could guarantee a "B" or better.

I have a great love for music although I'm not a musician and so it is only natural to attempt rhyme, rhythm and metre in my writing.

My craft, if one could call it that, has been self taught, often taking what I feel is the appropriate style from Poets I admire. Thus you may see shades of Robert Service, Edgar Guest, James Riley, Tennyson or Longfellow in my verse. I often seek a punch line or surprise ending.

I lean towards ballads and attempts at humor. Once I've chosen a theme I love to let my mind run rampant.

I'm 80 years old now so perhaps my style etc. seems a bit antiquated. I have a collection of over 400 of my own verses written at various periods in my life. Mostly I've written for self satisfaction. I have been published but most sparingly.

I have belonged to verse writing groups in Iowa and Oregon and found this participation stimulating. I spent several years in contact with a niece in Iowa who was taking a course in writing children's literature. It proved to be a very interesting correspondence. I have her writing which I treasure.

I'm sure I would enjoy an exchange of work and promise not to offer any criticism that you do not ask for, and I shall try to make my part interesting.

Don't worry about spelling or writing; I am terrible. To me it's the thoughts that count.

I lived as a young man through the Depression, served in WWII, worked various occupations, and love reading. I've been a political animal, a union activist, and a Sunday school teacher. I love to debate (argue) and must confess that I am opinionated.

If I am fortunate enough to participate in this program I shall do my best.

Ralph

THE REUNION

Aunt May sat in her rocking chair
And glared at people everywhere
John passed out beer or orange or cokes
And told his usual old stale jokes
Ezra touted from the Books
And gave the beer boys dirty looks
Will then read his latest verse

'Bout Granma falling from the Hearse
It took them several hours to find
The body they had left behind

Daisy modeled Grampa's clothes
Tim tripped her up, broke her nose
Jimmy bobbed off Nellie's curls
And chased the other little girls
Tim shot Pete out of the tree
Where he had climbed to better see
Alice drowned but who should care
She'd oft' been told not to go there

May guffoed when Sally sang
With that fake old country twang
Sally finally slapped May's face
Their hit and run fight was a race
Steve ripped his pants, Mike tore his shirt
As they lay scuffling in the dirt
For Steve was Sally's pride and joy
And Mike was May's oldest boy

Considering these things all and all
We really truly had a ball

I feel this is a fair example of my Ballad form of humor.

I was very sorry I was unable to get a humorous punch line in the third stanza.

Do you like this?

CARDIAC SURGERY

Silence—
My drug filled brain
Reviews events
Resulting in
My presence here.

Movement—
Hot surgical lights
piercing eye lids—
Gowned attendants
Everywhere.

A sigh—
A mask descends
Silencing lips—
Whispering—Whispering
A silent prayer.

Consciousness fades
Accepting HEART REPAIR
or OBLIVION
For me lying there.

"OH LORD—MY GOD—"

I recently underwent cardiac surgery.
Do you find blank verse interesting? I seldom attempt it.
Does verse two adequately express the movement to the surgical room?
Does [verse] three express sounds, or the whispering of the silent prayer?
Does verse 4 adequately express the risk involved?
Do you think the final line in quotes is appropriate?

Ralph seeks Crystal's advice and encourages her to critique his poems. Crystal tries to answer each of Ralph's questions; she gives a longer response than is typical of most eighth-grade partners:

Dear Ralph,

Hi, my name is Crystal. I am a freshman at Moscow Jr. High school. This is my second year of participating in writing partners. I enjoy writing but have never won any awards.

I am an active member in Job's Daughters. I play in band, I really enjoy art, and am also participating on the *Ursa Major* team. *Ursa Major* is a junior high magazine that ranks as one of the highest in the nation.

This week I am sending you a story I wrote in English class. I would really appreciate it if you would tell me what you think of it, and tell me what I could do to improve my story.

Ralph I really loved "The Reunion." It was really funny and I enjoyed it thoroughly. It was perfectly fine that there was no punch line at the end of stanza 3. It flowed very well!

"Cardiac Surgery" must have been very difficult for you to write! It was really descriptive. Yes, the blank verse was very appropriate. I thought it fit wonderfully. Verse 2 was exceptionally good, it showed very well the movement in the operating room. The 3rd line was a bit confusing but still very acceptable. Verse 4 describes very well the risk involved when under going surgery.

Yours truly,
Crystal

P.S. There is no need to send back any of my writings, would you like me to send back yours?

Crystal includes a long story that begins as follows:

The Great Journey

A long time ago in a far away land, lived a young boy who went by the name of Thio. He went by this name because his real name was Farmeetio T. Roedensack III. His father was a kind man who worked as a blacksmith, in the small town of Kensorck.

Thio had a dream of sailing across the great oceans, and to discover new lands. Thio's father, Farmeetio, wanted Thio to be a blacksmith as he had become. As long as Thio stayed in this small town he knew his dreams would never come true.

The next morning before daylight Thio set out to find the ocean shore. He knew the journey would take him days, but he was determined. One day passed and Thio was still in high spirits. So again he set off, but this time a little later in the day.

[On his way to the coast Thio spends a night in a barn where he is cared for by the beautiful Isabelle who is tending animals. After months of travel and work, Thio buys a boat and sets sail, only to be shipwrecked in a storm. He survives by eating coconuts, but is captured by a vicious tribe that puts him over a fire. The fire burns his ropes and he is free, whereupon he returns to his homeland, finds and marries Isabelle, and lives a happy life.]

In response to her story, Ralph gives Crystal some of the feedback she requests. Less certain than Ron in the mentoring role and with less background in literary theory, Ralph places himself clearly in the position of fellow author by sharing some of his struggles with prose. He also makes constructive suggestions based on his own experience as a reader and writer and challenges his partner to experiment by showing her some of his own "playing around" with verse.

Dear Fellow Writer:

Your story, "The Great Journey," does show promise. I'm sure if you're pursuing this craft you may some day find yourself published.

You requested my criticism and comments. If I were to have written this I would have used the words "One morning" instead of "The next morning" due to the general time frame of the preceding opening.

I like your use of conversation. I always had trouble with this and still do.

The change of pronouns in the second paragraph is a fault I used to struggle with when I first started writing. Also I had trouble changing from past to present rather indiscriminately.

Remember, "We learn to do by doing" and success results "in making one's *good* better and one's *better* best." As indicated these phrases in quotes are of others.

I really enjoyed your letter of introduction. My two daughters went through the chairs in Rainbow and two of my grand daughters went thru the chairs in Job's Daughters.

I don't know what *Ursa* is but it does sound interesting

I'm glad you do not wish return of your work as I am keeping a file of our exchanges. You needn't return my work either as I am keeping a copy of it in this file as well,

Might I suggest that if you are seriously interested in writing prose that you read 0. Henry? He was a great short story writer.

Ralph

Happy Thanksgiving

I'm responding rather quickly as I feel that perhaps a late start has robbed us of some of our exchange time.

Ralph attaches to his letter a poem with a piece of paper with the following instructions taped over the introductory "assignment":

Please read this poem before removing this cover.
Does it make much sense?
Now read the concealed introduction.
Does it make the poem more complete?
Does it rob the poem of its mystic quality?
Would you prefer that this be told in the more conventional verse?
Would you like to have some fun? If so, take this theme of a man, say in his 60s, and a young girl that are known to each other only through written communication and write a story for me. It could be a girl that answers a letter of a war buddy of her father's, the father having died. It could be a Sunday school girl writing a shut-in whom she never meets. It could end in meeting, a disappointment, or in death of one of the parties. However you chose to develop it I'm sure that I would find it interesting.

HIDDEN FLOWERS

I marvel at the beauty I find in you
Hidden by the foliage that others view
The world knows not
If it be peaceful slumber
Shy exotic dream
Or sorrow for your loneliness
That bows your head

When you dance in full bloom loveliness
Displaying your beauty to all of us
The world knows not
If caused by recent rain
Bright sunshine

Gentle breeze
This bright and joyous living
Stemming from the root of you.

Ah little flower introduced by chance
Hidden from me by circumstance
Admired for the messages you send
Admired for the beauty that be you
Unknown to the world at large
So like another flower
I nurtured to full blown loveliness
As now together you bloom
In memory's garden of happiness.

This first verse is a sample of my early work. Note the simplicity of it. Later I was to write some pretty heavy stuff on the subject of WW II and the Vietnam struggle.

OF WAR

Floating gently 'cross the heavens
Sitting on a cloud
Looking down on field and meadow
I felt so strong and proud
Saw an army down there fighting
Screams of dying rang aloud
Sadness then replaced elation
Sat I then with shamed head bowed

In this second verse I borrowed the theme from the famous poem "The Gingham Dog and the Calico Cat" by Eugene Field. But I took them off the mantel and hung them over the clothesline with the same results and then added my own bit of sarcasm. What do you think? Is this sort of sick humor?

JIMMY'S LOSS

Jimmy had this fighting cat
Mean until the day
He tied him on the clothes line
With Pup—a dirty grey
No one knows unto this day
What came of cat or pup
But confidently my friend
They ate each other up
Since then our Jim's been very sad
He longs for pup and cat
To hang them on the clothesline
And that my friend is that

Of course I could not publish this as my own original theme but it was fun writing it.

Like Ron, Ralph explains the context of each piece, what inspired it, the structure, and so on. Crystal, like Joe, responds to Ralph's challenge to write a story; perhaps a romantic, she changes the age of the man considerably:

Dear Ralph,

I'm glad you wrote back so quickly, I really enjoy this exchanging of writing! "Hidden Flowers" made sense before I read the introduction, but was even more so after. Definitely not, I think the poem still has its mystic quality. On "The War" I think the simplicity of it gives it the right touch. I loved "Jimmy's Loss" it was really funny, it made me laugh! It sounded like it would have been fun to write.

I decided to take your challenge. I wrote about a girl in her 20s and she gets in touch with a soldier in World War Two. Well, you'll find out the rest when you read it. It is still really scratchy. I'm not sure if I like it or not.

Yours Truly,
Crystal

A few years ago in the town of Chicago, a girl by the name of Sharrel joined a group of other girls. They wanted to send soldiers fighting in the war some hope, something to look forward to. They sent letters to the soldiers, and continued to keep in touch over the years until the war ended.

One day a soldier arrived at her home and asked for her. Sharrel came to the door and could not believe her eyes, the soldier's name was Greg. You see, he was madly in love with Sharrel even though they had never met.

The problem was, Sharrel was already engaged to be married. She decided to pretend to not be engaged, and keep Greg's hopes up.

Derral, Sharrell's fiancé, didn't like the whole idea and refused to cooperate. So she decided to tell Greg the truth, but couldn't do it. That meant she had to pretend to like Greg for three days.

Greg and Sharrel went out that night, and her friend recognized her. So Sharrel had to explain the whole problem to her.

By the second day Sharrel was falling in love with Greg, even though she was already spoken for. But she refused to allow it.

On the third day Sharrel knew she was in love with Greg and told Derral the truth. He was furious and left the house

in a rage. So Greg and Sharrel got married the following
year and lived happily ever after.

I do need to develop it more! But other than that do you like it?
What should I do to improve it. Remember be truthful!

Crystal is not afraid to send what is clearly a draft, a story-in-the-making.
She intends to work on this story, and wants Ralph's honest advice, which he
gives—not as a literary critic but as a reader. Perhaps because Crystal has
taken this risk, Ralph is willing to take one of his own by sending Crystal some
prose he had written when he was in high school; he expresses his own uncer-
tainty frankly.

To: Cris, Oct. 31
From: Ralph

Dear Fellow Writer:

Thank you for your promptness in writing. I realize that your story is not
a finished product. But I also realize that you were eager to respond to
the challenge I gave you.

Not being a prose writer I feel a bit inadequate to be offering constructive criticism, but here goes.

The similarity in the names Darrel and Sherral tended to be confusing to me. I half expected a play on words or names, later in the story.

In Par. 5 you introduced another female character or at least I
thought you did. I expected to see her as the tattle tale. Perhaps she had
a crush on Derral.

Three days is rather a short time, rather a rapid scenario for all that
takes place, but then they have been corresponding for some time. But
love is love.

0. Henry, a very successful short story writer, had a knack for making old themes interesting with a surprise ending at or near the end.

He might have written this sort of ending—"Derral marries the mystery
girl, Greg marries Sherral the next year. The following year both couples
get a divorce and Derral and Sherral celebrate by getting hitched."

It is only fair that I give you an example of my prose.

My disregard for punctuation often left my prose fuzzy. Maybe that is
why I switched to verse where I take full advantage of poetic license.

Please be as frank in your analysis of "The First Snowfall" as I have
been with you.

Ralph

*Written as a junior in high school. Junior was our 3rd year of high
school. High school consisted of 9th, 10th, 11th, and 12th grades.*

FIGURE 7-1

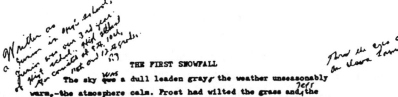

THE FIRST SNOWFALL

The sky was a dull leaden gray, the weather unseasonably
warm,-the atmosphere calm. Frost had wilted the grass and the
fallen piles of leaves- brown - curled and dead. Trees, bushes,
and flowers- shorn of their summer splendor stood like ghostly shadows
of their former selves, against the dirty sky.

Man had aided frost in the feilds. All the glory of growth was
gone. A havoac of destruction was all that remained. Dead fields stretched
out to the horizon- black and scarred by fire or plow,-or shorn and mangled -
by harvester or husker.

Flys and creeping insects had been silenced. Birds were gone too,
from the trees, and fields. The flocks and herds, had left had left the
the wilted meadows, and stood quietly in the yards. A late flock of
geese wavered like a farewell flag across the murky sky.

From farm houses in the distance, long thin scrolls of smoke
rose lazily upward, to be lost at last in the sky. It was a haunting scene —
depressive, depressive and saddening. Yet within it all was cast an
undercurrent of feeling, a feeling of a great drama about to take place.

Then slowly, almost lazily, the first snow flakes descended.
They drifted down from heaven like large petals of flowers; increasing
until the air was full of them. Their coming was noiseless and peaceful.
Each seeming predestined, they settled down to take their places.

They covered the fields, the trees, the grasses and flowers.
They filled each crevess with a soft blanket of white- a soft virgin
blanket-tucking nature in as though it were a small child for the coming
months of rest. I was filled with the wonder, the beauty, the joy,
the comfort and the peace .

As I stood in reverie, the clouds, their duty done, drifted
apart. Evening had quickly descended. A lone evening star appeared
upon the horizon "Star light, Star bright, First star Ive seen tonight
Wish I may wish I might"—

The First Snowfall

The sky was a dull leaden gray—the weather unseasonably warm, the atmosphere calm. Frost had wilted the grass and left the fallen piles of leaves—brown—curled and dead. Trees, bushes, and flowers—shorn of their summer splendor stood like ghostly shadows of their former selves, against the dirty sky.

Man had aided frost in the fields. All the glory of growth was gone. A havoc of destruction was all that remained. Dead fields stretched out to the horizon—black and scarred by fire or plow, or shorn and mangled by harvester or husker.

Flies and creeping insects had been silenced. Birds were gone too, from the trees, and fields. The flocks and herds had left, had left the wilted meadows, and stood quietly in the yards. A late flock of geese wavered like a farewell flag across the murky sky.

From farm houses in the distance, long thin scrolls of smoke rose lazily upward, to be lost at last in the sky. It was a haunting scene—depressive, depressive and saddening. Yet within it all was cast an undercurrent of feeling, a feeling of a great drama about to take place.

Then slowly, almost lazily, the first snow flakes descended. They drifted down from heaven like large petals of flowers, increasing until the air was full of them. Their coming was noiseless and peaceful. Each seeming predestined, they settled down to take their places.

They covered the fields, the trees, the grasses and flowers. They filled each crevice with a soft blanket of white—a soft virgin blanket—tucking nature in as though it were a small child for the coming months of rest. I was filled with the wonder, the beauty, the joy, the comfort and the peace.

As I stood in reverie, the clouds, their duty done, drifted apart. Evening had quickly descended. A lone evening star appeared upon the horizon. "Star light, Star bright, First star I've seen tonight, Wish I may, wish I might. . . ."

I wrote this during an Economics class. English was my next class. We were studying American literature.

Happy Halloween. Hope you have a low sugar level.

I love little notes. Do you? I guess it's 'cause I write for pleasure.

"The First Snowfall": I thought of adding a school boy, coat open, dinner pail swinging, dreaming of sleds, skates, & Santa. Do you think that would have added to this or did I chose the right stopping place? Perhaps I should have added the morn after with the virgin blanket marked only by a Rabbit's tracks in the snow.

Would you have had the persosn on a hill? Most of all do you think this has a poetic flow, I tried so hard to develop this??

Unfortunately, their fall partnership is short and the end of the semester comes quickly. Crystal does not answer all Ralph's questions. But as Ralph has shared an attempt at her genre, Crystal matches risk for risk and tries poetry:

Dear Ralph,

It was really nice to see you at my installation. [Ralph's granddaughters are Job's Daughters in the same town.] Do you think it went well? I think it went pretty well.

Sorry it has taken me so long to write you back, I have been incredibly busy! With my term for Job's Daughter's and with school, I'm having trouble finding time to write. I'll just have to make it up to you!

I thought your last writing was absolutely wonderful. I enjoyed every minute that I spent reading it.

One of the writings that I am sending you is about depression. Although I promise you I'm not depressed. The second writing you are receiving is about a young girl trapped in the middle of a forgotten children's story book.

I do hope that you will enter your "Hidden Flowers" poem [in the Writing Partners anthology], I think that was my favorite. Or maybe you should send in your poem "The War." That poem was so wonderful, it made me think about how painful war is.

Yours truly,
Crystal

DEPRESSION

Cold, alone.

Staring at the floor.

Secluded, stressed.

Left to hear your self-bashing thoughts.

Scared, silent.

Staring at the floor.

THE BOOK

Shallee was a young princess whose beauty reigned over all. A jealous widow wished that she could be as beautiful as Shallee. The widow went to a witch and had her cast a spell on Shallee. This spell made it so that when she found true love she would become trapped in a story book. The spell could only be broken if a little girl fell in love with the princess Shallee.

Three hundred years went by and the book had still never been read. Shallee was loosing hope.

Until a homeless man found this little book in a garbage dumpster. The man took the little book to his daughter Christy for Christmas. This was Christy's first Christmas present.

Christy was the happiest little girl in the whole world for that one moment. This book meant more to Christy than a million dollars would to a greedy man. Fortunately for Shallee, Christy would have fallen in love with her whether the story was good or not.

After about four days Shallee was released from the book's grasp. Christy was happy for the princess but had lost her only book. The words were still there but she could not read. Unfortunately, the pictures had left with Shallee. So the princess drew in the pictures for little Christy.

Shallee left that day and had nothing, she was in a strange place in a strange time. Even though the odds were against her she managed to get a job at a modeling company. After about two months Shallee got enough money to rent an apartment. She then went and found Christy and her father and asked them to move in with her.

Shallee and Christy's father fell in love and got married. They all lived together happily ever after.

Christy grew up and became famous writing children's books.

THE END

Dec. 5th.

Dear Crystal,

Sorry I did not stay to meet you after your Installation. Even though I was not up to par that day I was determined to be in attendance. I was duly impressed, as usual. The ceremony as usual was inspiring. The floor work, singing and dress— each time I see it it seems to touch a new chord. I could not help feeling a kinship with you. You join a host of other Job and Rainbow girls that are a pleasant part of my memories.

"Depression" showed great promise. The strength of it is in the choice of words. Do you like experimenting with poetry?

I liked "The Book" too. You seem to be getting a lot more into your work. I hope that I can feel a certain amount of credit for what inspiration I instill in you. Your youth showed in your romantic creations. Although I must confess my recent romance at 79 was not cold contemplation of having a care taker for my evening period of life. [A widower,

Ralph fell in love and married the year before his partnership with Crystal.]

I look forward to meeting you soon.

The enclosed poem will probably be my last contribution before we meet. It is rather lengthy. It was shorter at first ending with "She was only a doll you know!" But somehow it seemed to leave the story unfinished. Do you think the latter part of the poem was worth extending it? Does the last verse portray that they had both grown much older? It might interest you to know that only recently have I submitted some of my work to publication and out of four submissions I have picked up one fifth place in contests. It's fun and I have quite a few poems to choose from. I do not fall for the "subscription to anthologies" but I do relish the competition. I have also received 3 honorable mentions.

See you soon.

Your writing Pal,
Ralph

THE BROKEN BOND

'Twas sunny the day that first they met
She showed him her birthday doll
Dressed to the nines of fashion
Fit to attend a ball.

They often met on sunny days
They'd stroll along the street
The conversation would center 'round
The little doll so sweet.

"Why doesn't she talk"? "Why doesn't she sing?"
"How come she doesn't grow?"
He would look down at that upturned face;
"She's only a doll you know."

He witnessed her hair grow fuzzy
The color fade from her face
Patches appear on the splendor
On bonnet, gown and lace,
Then one day the stroller upset
And there upon the walk
The dolly lay with her head all smashed
Shocked he could not talk.

He felt her soft little hand in his
She spoke so sweet and low
"Lets not have a funeral. OK?
She's was only a dolly you know."
He stooped and gathered the pieces up

And put them in a sack
She righted the stroller and sped away
She never once looked back.

He never saw the child again
Perhaps she had moved away
Yet he could not forget that little doll
And that one eventful day
He went to a dollhouse; had it restored
Even gave it a name
But child's intuition was stronger than his
It never could be the same.

He heard her approach, adjust her step
To his grown short and slow
She smiled down at his weathered face
"Twas more than the doll, you know."

Crystal and her mother were among the first to arrive at the reception that December; she was eager to meet her most unique partner who had become a friend.

Elder partners, like Ralph, are priceless, for they show their young partners that writing can be immensely pleasurable all one's life. (Studies show that age has no effect on creativity, as Ralph's writing so clearly demonstrates.) And they help break stereotypes of elders young people may have acquired.

Dear Melanie,

How nice that you are learning to knit—I am chagrined to reveal that I do not knit, or crochet, but so admire those who do. Nor do I like to sew, although most grandmas are very good at these particular hobbies. My two daughters are adept at these arts, but woe is me, I am not! Nor am I apt to take up any of these creative skills. . . .

Since his partnership with Crystal, Ralph has had other partners, all of whom have been as delighted with his poems as Crystal. These younger writers have not only been entertained and inspired, but have also been given a chance to learn about other times and places, a chance to go outside their generation and view the world through an elder's eyes. And this is one of the most important rewards of having a writing partner, being able to learn about another writer, a little bit of what makes her laugh, love, despair; her obsessions, principles, beliefs; the significant events or people that give her life meaning—the things that make her write. No literature anthology or even "collected works" can do this in quite the same way.

8

In Conclusion

it will not matter if your pockets are empty
if you write with a green Bic or a black Bic
or the blood of your finger
you will write
you will write

Ruth Forman, "If You Lose Your Pen"

P*eople* in the community need not be scholars, teachers, or professionals to be effective writing coaches, mentors, or simply companions for young writers. They need not share a common set of beliefs about what is good or bad in literature, or adhere to any pedagogy of expository or creative writing. A drive to write and a respect for that drive in other, less experienced writers are all that is required. Ralph, Ron, Lindy, Saundra, Chance, Ken, and the other community and college writers included in these chapters delight in their work; they are people who take pleasure in *giving* writing to their partners, as one might give a gift, hoping for but asking for nothing in return. Peter Elbow writes that

> The essential human act at the heart of writing is the act of *giving*. There's something implacable and irreducible about it: handing something to someone because you want her to have it, not asking for anything in return, and if it is a gift of yourself—as writing always is—risking that she won't like it or even accept it. Yet though giving can sound rare and special if you rhapsodize about it, it is of course just a natural and spontaneous human impulse. (1981,20)

Perhaps this act of giving characterizes writing partners' exchanges best. For beneath the questions—"tell me how I can improve this," "does this part make sense?"—is the gift itself: "look what I wrote!" "Enjoy reading it as much as I enjoyed writing it and as much as I take pleasure in giving it to you." The family newsletters sold for a nickel, Barbara's "Kisses That Clicked," the short story I sent to *American Girl,* the plays neighborhood children invent and perform—these are gifts of writing.

Elbow is right when he claims that "This central act of giving is curiously neglected in most writing instruction" (21); in school, students share writing with each other and the teacher, but rarely do they simply *give* it to others for their pure pleasure in reading. Sharing, even in workshop, usually has a purpose—to solicit feedback for revision, to learn more about audiences, to judge whether one has accomplished one's goal. Possibly, this is one reason why the writing people do in schools is viewed differently than the playful writing they do outside school; in school, giving the reader a story, poem, book report, or essay solely for the simple pleasure in giving is rare. Because writing partners choose their work and share it voluntarily, the element of gift-giving is always there:

> Here's a piece I wrote for history that I thought you might enjoy.

> This is kind of an odd piece. Oh well. Have fun!

> P. S. I hope you like the poem.

> I hope you enjoy my story.

> I hope you like it!

> P. S. You can keep my writing, too, if you would like to.

> I'm sending you another poem I wrote. It's about my mom. I was going to give it to her for Christmas but I thought she deserved more than a poem.

> It will be nice to know that someone will be reading what I have written.

> This week I am sending two short poems, my two favorite I might add.

Partners also seem to accept writing *as* gifts:

> I am an avid reader, so receiving your writing will be a pleasure.

> I made a copy of your story.

> Thanks for letting me read your work.

How often do we *thank* a writer for the chance to read his work? How often do we thank our students for sharing writing with us? How often in a classroom do writers thank each other? "Let my writing please you," these writers say, "let my 'treasure' be yours." In Writing Partners, even writing that originally was done for a class assignment, for a teacher, for a grade, becomes a present, given for no other reason than to delight the writing partner. By asking them to give their work freely for the edification of readers, Writing Partners, like literary magazines or other publications, places writers in a different relationship to their work—one that emphasizes the reader *as* reader (not evaluator) and writer *as* writer (not student). The lines between "school writing" and "writing for fun" become less distinct.

Also more blurry are the lines between writing as work and writing as play. Writing for the sheer joy of it, giving writing as a gift, and reading to delight in someone's words do not preclude risk-taking, critical reading, revision; the intense love of writing and desire to give it inspire hard work. Authors who continue a partner's story, attempt unrhymed poetry, or dare to share an imperfect piece—are true writers who care deeply about their audiences, who labor because they want to say something exactly right, make readers laugh, cry, think. It never occurred to me, as I listened to my father pound the typewriter keys, that his midnight labor was part of the love of creating. And perhaps that is why I never wanted to be a writer; I never saw the connection. "What an opportunity," a community writer once wrote about the project, "and what an education for the young people. I didn't even consider being a writer until I was out of school."

I hope that you will take away from this book a sense of the potential of writing partnerships to build bridges between students and their communities, and strengthen the bonds that all writers share—the love of shaping ideas, the impulse to move readers, and the courage to explore. I hope the letters and writing I have included in this book will inspire you to find partners for your own students—one, two, a dozen. . . . Start simply, expand the project as time and energy allow. If you do begin a project, I would welcome hearing from you (you can reach me through the Department of English, University of Idaho, Moscow, Idaho 83844-1102). Writing this book has been my pleasure. I have learned about myself as a writer, entered the worlds of other writers, and acquired a deeper respect for the work writers do. Most of all, I have discovered just how much writing means to so many people. That, by itself, is some reward.

APPENDIX

Letter for Parents and Permission Form

Dear Parent or Guardian,

Your child has volunteered to participate in the Writing Partners Project. In this program, young writers in selected schools who want to participate are paired with writers in the Moscow community for the purpose of exchanging and responding to writing. The aim of the Writing Partners Project is to give younger writers a wider audience and support for their writing, and to help them see that their writing is important and interesting to other writers outside the school. It is also designed to foster a larger community of writers—people of all ages who take pleasure in writing and share many of the same struggles and successes. Here is how the Writing Partners Project works:

If you give permission for your child to participate, please read and sign the attached "Parent Permit" form and return it to your child's English teacher. Your son/daughter should sign the "Student Writing Partners' Responsibilities" sheet and return that as well. Once the forms are returned, your child will be assigned a writing partner from the Moscow community. This person will be either a student in a writing course at the University of Idaho, or another adult who has been selected to participate in the program. The university student partners are enrolled in Writing Workshop for Teachers, a course designed to introduce prospective secondary English and elementary teachers to a variety of writing activities and classroom approaches to the teaching of writing. Other University of Idaho student partners may come from upper-level writing courses. Writing partners from the nonuniversity community are people who write regularly and enjoy sharing and talking about writing; they are selected according to the guidelines attached.

Following receipt of signed "Parent Permit" and "Student Writing Partners' Responsibilities" form signed by your child, your son or daughter's English teacher and I will pair your child with a university or community writer. (While I will attempt to pair writers on the basis of their general writing interest, I cannot guarantee a perfect match, nor can I guarantee a partner of a certain age or sex.) Your child will then receive a letter from her or his writing partner, along with some writing the partner wishes to share. The writing may be poetry, personal reminiscence, fiction, or essay, depending on the interests of the writer. Your child should respond with a letter of introduction that includes reactions to the partner's writing and some original writing that your child wants to share with his or her partner. The writing your child sends may be writing done for school (book responses, essays, poetry) or outside school. It may be writing in progress and in draft form, so long as it is legible. In addition, I encourage partners to include questions about their writing that they would like their partners to answer. (Partners should return each other's writing, but to be on the safe side, writers are advised to keep copies of the writing they send.) The partners are not to be critics or editors or tutors. Instead, they are interested readers who will share nonjudgmental responses and reactions.

For the duration of the project—the university semester—partners exchange and respond to each other's writing regularly. All writing and letters are to be exchanged through the teachers and me. Student partners will turn in all writing and letters for their community writers to their teachers; I collect them and pass them along to the community partners. Similarly, I collect the writing from the partners and take them to the teachers, who pass them along to the students. Partners do not meet until the end of the semester and should communicate for no other purpose than to share and respond to writing. Partners should not send their writing through e-mail or to home addresses; all writing and letters must go through your child's English teacher and through me. I may read your child's letters and writing as well as the material the community writers share. I do this so that I may keep informed as to how the activity is going. On some occasions, the partner may wish to share your child's writing with others; if your child wishes his or her writing to be read by no one but me and the partner, he or she should let us know and we will respect his or her wishes. In addition, I may use some of your child's writing and/or letters to the partner in presentations or publications about the project. If so, I will use the writing only in a positive context, and will not cite the writer's full name. *Your signature on the permission form and your child's signature on the "Student Writing Partners' Responsibilities" form constitute permission for me to quote from your child's writing in presentations and/or publications about the project. If you approve of your child's participation in the project but do not want me to quote from her or his writing as described, please write a note to that effect on the permit form.*

At the end of the project, the University of Idaho Writing Workshop for Teachers class will produce an anthology of writing submitted by students and their partners in each school. The anthologies will be available at cost;

there is no obligation to buy one. Also, we will host a reception at the end of the term so that all the writers may meet each other, receive their anthologies, and celebrate their work. Details on the reception are forthcoming. In addition, I will distribute project evaluation forms at the end of the semester for you and your son or daughter so that I may continue to refine and improve the project. But I welcome your input at any time.

Your child's participation is strictly voluntary and will have no effect on his or her school grade. He or she may stop participating at any time. However, I ask that students who do participate make a commitment to send writing to their partners regularly and respond in a timely fashion. The experience is designed to be fun, but it is above and beyond the student's regular school work, and there are no guaranteed benefits from participation. Let me know if you have any questions. Thank you.

Sincerely,
Candida Gillis, Project Director
Department of English, University of Idaho

I have read the attached description of the Writing Partners Project and give my permission for my son/daughter to participate.

Child's name: _____

(Please print)

Signature of parent or legal guardian:

_____

Phone # (optional): _____

Date: _____

REFERENCES

Atwell, Nancie. 1987. *In the Middle.* Portsmouth, NH: Boynton/Cook.

Calkins, Lucy McCormick. 1994. *The Art of Teaching Writing.* Portsmouth, NH: Heinemann.

Davis, Chris. 1995. "The I-Search Paper Goes Global: Using the Internet as a Research Tool." *English Journal* 84 (6): 27–33.

Elbow, Peter. 1981. *Writing With Power.* New York: Oxford University Press.

Forman, Ruth. 1993a. "If You Lose Your Pen." In *We Are the Young Magicians*, 12–13. Boston: Beacon.

————.1993b. "Poetry Should Ride the Bus." In *We are the Young Magicians*, 10–11. Boston: Beacon.

Gillis, Candida. 1992. *The Community as Classroom.* Portsmouth, NH: Boynton/Cook.

Graves, Donald. 1983. *Writing: Teachers & Children at Work.* Portsmouth, NH: Heinemann.

King, Laurie, & Dennis Stoval, eds. 1992. *Classroom Publishing.* Hillsboro, OR: Blue Heron.

McFarland, Ron. 1993a. "Fishing the Last Light." *Timberline* I (Winter): 12–13.

————.1993b. *The Haunting Familiarity of Things.* 1993. Canton, CT: Singular Speech Press.

————.1994. "The Apology." *Tomorrow Magazine* 12:28.

————.1995. "Why I Love Baseball." *Aethlon* 13 (Fall): 86.

————.1996. *The World of David Wagoner.* Moscow: University of Idaho Press.

Noden, Harry. 1995. "A Journey Through Cyberspace: Reading and Writing in a Virtual School." *English Journal* 84 (6): 19–26.